OIL AND DEMOCRACY IN IRAQ

Oil and Democracy in Iraq

Robert Springborg (lead author)
Clement Henry
Massoud Karshenas
Roger Owen
Mona Said
John Sfakianakis

SAQI

in association with

**LONDON
MIDDLE EAST
INSTITUTE
SOAS**

ISBN (10): 0-86356-665-0
ISBN (13): 978-0-86356-665-3

Manufactured in the United Kingdom by CPI

SAQI
26 Westbourne Grove, London W2 5RH
825 Page Street, Suite 203, Berkeley, California 94710
Tabet Building, Mneimneh Street, Hamra, Beirut
www.saqibooks.com

in association with

The London Middle East Institute
School of Oriental and African Studies, Russell Square, London WC1H 0XG
www.lmei.soas.ac.uk

Contents

Preface

Oil has played an enormously important role in the political economy of Iraq and is likely to continue to do so in the future. Its borders and inclusion of a large non-Arab, Kurdish population in the North reflect the distribution of oil fields discovered in Mesopotamia before and after WWI. The rapid accumulation of oil revenues from the 1950s contributed to the revolution of 1958 by stimulating economic dislocation, by further widening the gap between rulers and ruled, by feeding corruption and by providing to nationalists a potent symbol of imperialist exploitation. The nationalization of the Iraqi oil industry in 1972, quickly followed by the first great oil boom, provided the rents with which Saddam Hussein and his Ba'thist colleagues constructed what became the most authoritarian state in the Arab world. Those same rents gave rise to the Dutch disease that gradually enervated the non-oil sectors of the economy, leaving the Ba'thist state steadily more dependent upon oil earnings until it ultimately collapsed with the invasion by US led forces in March 2003.

Nor does the story end there. One reason given for the invasion itself was that certain US decision makers saw in the control of Iraqi oil a dramatic means of reasserting American influence over global energy markets. With 11 per cent of the world's proven oil reserves – the second largest after Saudi Arabia's extraordinary quarter share – Iraq is sitting on more than \$3.5 trillion worth of oil at the price obtaining in January 2004.[1]

But the potential value of Iraqi oil is not just that it can add significantly to currently overstretched global supplies and while so doing enrich numerous actors involved in its exploitation. Of potentially even greater impact on the global energy system would be the bold adoption by Iraq of a decisive new model for its oil industry. It was Iraq, after all, that played a signal role for the Third World in nationalizing its oil industry while most similar ones were still under the dominant influence of international oil companies (IOCs). Part and parcel of economic globalization that has swept the world since the end of the Cold War, neo-liberal economic reforms have been conspicuous in their near absence in Third World energy sectors. In most, the dominant role of the state, exerted through ministries and state owned national oil companies (NOCs), has been amended and reduced, but principally downstream, away from the vital upstream supplies where more and more of the profits are made.

The continued reluctance of Third World producers to subject their energy sectors to neo-liberal reforms is deemed by many adherents of the Washington Consensus in favour of those reforms

---

1.   David C. Nagel, 'Iraq and its Oil – A Longer-term Perspective' (2 January 2004), private communication. Husain al-Shahristani, Deputy Speaker of the National Assembly, claimed at a conference on 1 July 2005 that Iraqi oil reserves were worth \$10 trillion. Iraqi Oil Wealth: Issues of Governance and Development, a conference held at the London School of Economics and jointly sponsored by the Open Society Institute.

to constitute the single largest obstacle to rapid expansion of world energy supplies, hence to be the principle cause of current high prices. So for many in Washington, including neo-conservatives in the Bush Administration, the great prize of the Iraqi oil industry was not just the liquid gold itself, but its dramatic privatization and then rapid expansion. Presumably by such means they hoped to induce widespread neo-liberal reforms, especially in the Gulf region, where large producers like Saudi Arabia and Kuwait have thus far only toyed with them.[1]

That the IOCs themselves – at least insofar as we know – did not jump on the bandwagon the neo-conservatives intended for Iraq, is suggestive of changes that have occurred not only to them, but to the world energy system as a whole.[2] The IOCs, historically dominated by American or British companies, have come to reflect the meaning of their name 'international' much more

---

1. According to the BBC 'Newsnight' programme of 16 March 2005, neo-conservatives in the Bush Administration, especially in the Department of Defence, starting planning to 'sell off' the Iraqi oil industry within weeks of Bush taking office. The plan that was adopted was then approved by Ahmad Chalabi 'shortly after the US entered Baghdad'. http://news.bbc.co.uk/1/hi/programmes/newsnight/4354269.stm Among the US think tanks advocating a thoroughgoing sell-off of Iraqi oil was The Heritage Foundation, which asserted that 'Privatization works everywhere' and 'oil privatization generates high economic efficiency and market capitalization.' Ariel Cohen and Gerald P. O'Driscoll, 'The Road to Economic Prosperity for a Post-Saddam Iraq,' The Heritage Foundation, Policy Research Paper, 1633 (24 June 2003).

2. The Pentagon's plan to sell off Iraqi oil fields was vigorously opposed by what the BBC refers to as 'a combination of Big Oil executives and US State Department pragmatists.' Chief among the former was former Shell Oil CEO, Philip Carroll, who was made responsible by the US Government for Iraqi oil production in April 2003. He claims to have informed Paul Bremer in May 2003 that 'There was to be no privatization of Iraqi oil resources or facilities while I was involved.' *Ibid.*

than previously. As they have globalized, their formerly intimate connections with the American and British governments have been diluted. Whereas twenty or thirty years ago the principals of such IOCs might have been willing to sign on to a US and UK government-led adventure in Iraq, as indeed they did in Iran, for example, in the 1950s, now they are much more cautious. None in fact have sought to ride their respective national coat-tails into key positions in Baghdad at present, patiently waiting for a legitimate national Iraqi government to emerge with which they can do business. Clearly they are fearful of moving too quickly and in tandem with the troops, lest they compromise their internationalist credentials or risk their capital in an insecure legal environment.

Globalization of the IOCs is mirrored by a similar trend among Third World NOCs, many of which have, like their much bigger IOC brothers, sought business outside what for them are increasingly only notional national borders. The most dramatic examples of these moves are takeovers or attempted takeovers, such as that recently sought by the Chinese National Offshore Oil Company (CNOOC) of the US company Unocal. But the more numerous ones are the increasingly normal, everyday business operations of such companies as Algeria's Sonatrach, which explores in Yemen and operates joint ventures in Lebanon, Egypt and further afield in Ecuador and Venezuela; and Abu Dhabi's National Petroleum Corporation, which among other activities has constructed platforms in Qatar.[1] Compelling for all is the strong positive correlation at the firm level between globalization and profitability. So, for example, the Kuwait Petroleum Corporation

---

1.   Randa Alami, 'Changing Financial Structures in the Arab World: Some Implications for Oil and Gas.' Oxford Institute for Energy Studies (April 2005), p. 39.

(KPC) has remained a strictly national enterprise, essentially serving as a cash cow for the Kuwaiti government. Its turnover in 1981 was about $25 billion, almost exactly the same annual figure in current dollars that it achieved in 2003. In the meantime BP, which achieved an almost identical figure to the KPC in 1981, lost control over oil in Iran, Kuwait and elsewhere and had to aggressively globalize and diversify to survive. By 2003 its turnover was some ten times what it had been in 1981. The lesson to globalize and diversify, or stagnate, is thus clear and well known. It is only the more retrograde of the national oil companies, with protected reserves, no competition and no incentives, that continue to operate entirely within their national horizons.

A lessening of the sharp historical differentiation between IOCs and NOCs as a result of globalization is mirrored in the growing complexity of relations between them, and in the legal and operational relationships through which oil is extracted, processed and sold. The traditional relationship between IOCs and producer countries was typically one in which the latter received royalties and taxes from the former in exchange for access to oil, which the IOC then marketed on its own account. Over time a variety of other, more complex relationships between producer countries and companies have emerged, including the widely used Production Sharing Agreement (PSA), in which in return for access to oil, companies provide percentages of oil produced to the countries, which they in turn market as they so desire. Driving the greater complexity of such commercial relationships is not only the higher value of the commodity itself and changing relationships of power between producer countries and IOCs, but the rising costs of extracting oil. High extraction costs in turn have demanded the creation of new financing mechanisms as oil company in-house sources and bank lending, the traditional sources, have had to be supplemented.[1]

Iraq is thus seeking to reconstitute its oil industry not only during a price boom, but when the global energy industry is being restructured through globalization, with uncertain results for its future. The old dichotomies between producer countries and IOCs, between IOCs and NOCs, and between suppliers and users of credit, are breaking down. Present high prices have rekindled a surge of resource nationalism on the part of producing countries, but they have also intensified pressure upon them to expand production and to do so through newly established, globalized mechanisms, many of which are formulated within neo-liberal, rather than nationalist perspectives. The Middle East and especially the Gulf, in which the global concentration of hydrocarbons is most intense, is the key focal point for these contending forces. Iraq is thus at the epicentre of global energy politics, precisely at the time when it is least well equipped to reach optimal decisions regarding its own national economic, political and social objectives, to say nothing of reconciling its national interests with international practices, concerns and pressures.

The magnitude of the challenge confronting Iraq is daunting. The physical state of its oil industry is parlous. War, sanctions and resource shortages – both human and physical – have taken

---

1. But Arab NOCs have been slow to mobilize new sources of capital. Only 23 oil and gas companies are currently listed on Arab stock exchanges, about 10 per cent of the total of 205 private oil and gas companies operating in the region. Bank capital thus remains disproportionately important for these operators, a fact reflecting the immaturity of capital markets in the region and the structure of the companies themselves. Nevertheless, 'Arab governments and NOCs can no longer exclusively rely on the intimacy of long-standing relations with IOCs or banks to secure funding.' See Alami, pp. 39–40, 53.

their toll. Current production is less than 2 million barrels per day, with exports struggling to hold steady at 1.5 mbd, as against production of 3.7 mbd in 1979, 3.5 mbd in 1990 and some 2.1–2.4 mbd in 2002.[1] Deputy Secretary of Defence Paul Wolfowitz boldly forecast to Congress in March 2003 that 'oil revenues of Iraq could bring between $50 and $100 billion over the course of the next two or three years.[2] The Coalition Provisional Authority (CPA) estimated that within a year Iraqi production would be back to 2.8–3 mbd.[3] In reality, many of the installations are so badly degraded that they are virtually beyond repair. Moreover, considerable damage has been done to several of Iraq's major oil fields by inappropriate exploitation practices in the final years of the Ba'thist regime.[4] While estimates of the cost of restoration of production to pre-war levels vary, a common figure is some $5–6 billion, with an additional $35–40 billion required to reach 5–6 mbd.[5] Estimates of production potential and the time taken to achieve it vary widely.[6] By the summer of 2005 some $2 billion

1. John S. Duffield, 'Oil and the Iraq War,' *The Middle East Review of International Affairs*, 9, 2 (23 June 2005), p. 10.

2. Cited in Gal Luft, 'Iraq's Oil Sector one Year After Liberation,' Saban Centre Middle East Memo #44 (17 June 2004).

3. *Ibid.*

4. Declining crude oil qualities and increased water cut from the Kirkuk field is probably due to over pumping just prior to the 2003 war. Other oil reservoirs appear to have been damaged by reinjection of excess fuel oil, refinery residue and gas-stripped oil. 'Iraq.' EIA Country Analysis Brief (November 2004).

5. Luft.

6. Duffield, p. 11, reviews various estimates, which range from those by the *Middle East Economic Survey* of it taking seven years to reach 4.5–6.0 mbd, to 6 mbd at the end of the decade by former Oil Minister Issam Chalabi; to 7 mbd over five years by former Undersecretary of oil Fadhil Chalabi, who, along with former Vice President and Director of the

had been spent in efforts to revive the oil sector, output within which was still falling, but according to some accounts, much of that money had been wasted on poor engineering works and corruption, or not spent at all.[1]

But even repair and maintenance of existing installations, to say nothing of development of new ones, has been rendered problematical by the insurgency, which has sought to cut the oil lifeline and thereby sever the primary artery of economic reconstruction. Insurgents have blown up pipelines, attacked loading terminals, sabotaged oilfield installations, and kidnapped or killed those employed in the industry, including the Director General of the Ministry of Petroleum.[2] At least 14,000 security

---

INOC, Tariq Shafiq, estimated that Iraq could easily reach 12 mbd.

1.   Khatoun Haidar, 'America Foundering Iraq's Economic Recovery,' *The Daily Star* (28 June 2005). Haidar singles out an expensive, underperforming water injection system for particular criticism, and cites the figure of $100 million as having been illegally transferred by the Oil Ministry into bank accounts in Jordan and Iraq. In May 2005 the Director of the largest oil production company, South Oil, Jabbar al-Uaibi, reported that production had declined below pre-war levels because his company lacked funds for 'essential maintenance and equipment.' BBC News, 24 May 2005. By January 2005 the Iraq Relief and Reconstruction Fund of $18.4 billion had designated $1.7 billion for reconstruction of oil infrastructure, of which $941 million had been obligated and $123 million expended. It was estimated by one source that in 2004 $4 billion was required for repairs, maintenance and operations of the oil infrastructure. See Duffield, p. 22.

2.   The impact of the insurgency on oil installations, as compared to the war, is indicated by the fact that 80 per cent of the damage occurred to it after military operations ceased and by the fact that oil production and exports grew steadily to 2.3 and 1.8 mbd respectively, by April 2004, at which time a decline commenced that has occasionally caused production to cease altogether. See Duffield, p. 20. Ali Hameed, Director General of the Ministry of Oil, was killed on May 19, 2005, as reported by BBC News.

personnel are dedicated to the task of protecting oilfields and pipelines, but even that small army is insufficient to prevent major interruptions, to say nothing of its inability to provide sufficient protection for aggressive refurbishment of installations.[1] The oil industry, which many thought would be the motor force for reconstruction, is not generating sufficient revenues for its own rehabilitation, much less that of the country as a whole.

The inadequacy of the legal, administrative and policy frameworks match the poor state of the infrastructural and security environments. No major IOC has deemed the transitional government as possessing sufficient legal status for it to enter into serious discussions about future contracts. A minimum estimate of the time required between the formation of the new constitutional government early in 2006, and clarification of 'the legal and regulatory questions about resource ownership required for big foreign oil companies to enter the market,' is 'more than a year.'[2] An Iraqi specialist at one such company estimated it would be 'three years before the operating environment is encouraging for majors.'[3] The dark cloud of pre-existing contracts signed with Russian, Chinese, French and other companies during the Saddam era, hangs over the legal status of much potentially lucrative Iraqi oil acreage. Conflicting signals about the validity of those contracts

1. By January 2005, only $123 million of the $1.7 billion allocated from the Iraq Relief and Reconstruction Fund for oil infrastructure had been spent. It was estimated then that in one year alone some $4 billion was needed for repairs, maintenance and operations. *Ibid.*, p. 22.

2. Neil MacDonald and Kevin Morrison, 'Iraqi Oil Output "Can Help Meet Rise in Demand", *Financial Times* (15 April 2005), p. 9. See also James Boxell, 'Oil Majors Take a Backseat,' *Financial Times* (14 April 2005), p. 23.

3. Interview, London, 25 June 2005.

arising in Iraq, combined with claims for their validity emanating from the capitals of the companies concerned, underscore the potential for a protracted legal imbroglio that would deter new suitors of Iraqi oil.

Present administrative arrangements are equally problematical. In the first instance, the administrative inheritance from the Ba'thists is not favourable. Unlike many other producers with nationalized oil industries, Iraq has thus far failed to differentiate administratively between the components of its industry. The first and primary such differentiation is between policy-making and commercial operations, with the former typically the preserve of the appropriate governmental ministry and the latter the responsibility of the national oil company. While Iraq has a Ministry of Oil and a national oil company, the former is intimately involved in the operations of the latter, more as a superior to a subordinate than as a policy maker to an executor of policy.[1]

The second important differentiation yet to be made in Iraq is within operations, typically by 'unbundling' the single national oil company into functional and/or geographic components, which persist as operational units within the single national company or are hived off as completely separate entities, sometimes to then be privatized. Such differentiation is at its very early stages in Iraq, where two major geographically determined companies (North and

---

1.   According to David Nagel, 'The Ministry should set national energy policy and production targets ... regulate the industry, license new acreage, lead negotiations at OPEC meetings as one of the core members, and act as non-executive chairman of INOC to avoid takeover by corrupt leadership.' For its part the INOC 'should be regarded as a quasi-private entity, required to achieve profitability. It should benchmark external competition, develop technical skills, pursue modern management practices, and build human resource capabilities, all pursuant to a sound long-term strategy.'

South) operate under the Iraqi National Oil Company (INOC), as do several functionally organized, mainly downstream ones. But the autonomy of these companies from the INOC is limited, much in the manner that its independence from the Ministry is circumscribed.

Various negative consequences flow from the comparative structural immaturity of the Iraqi oil industry. Unlike other countries with shorter histories of production and far less reserves, Iraq does not have a plethora of service companies, either public or private, specialized in various upstream and downstream operations. In Algeria, for example, such companies, largely government owned, have been commercialized. In competition with external companies and themselves induced to operate internationally, they have been forced to become technically proficient and cost effective. No component of the Iraqi oil industry has ever competed for contracts outside its own border, or within them for that matter, so one of the oldest and largest national oil industries is an increasing anomaly in the steadily more globalized world of oil. One manifestation of this relative backwardness is the failure of Iraq to keep pace with human skill development in the industry, a goal that was rendered difficult because of sanctions and isolation after 1991, but which was also impeded under Saddam and continues to be because of the administrative structure within which Iraqis work, whether as technicians or policy makers.

At a more prosaic level, the lack of functional differentiation impedes effective policy formation and implementation, as the two become intertwined and the latter directly subject to political considerations. One manifestation of this inappropriate complexity is lack of transparency, and therefore corruption.

Under Saddam such corruption was both financial and political, the latter reflecting the use of contracts to influence various countries' policies toward Iraq, especially in the final years of the regime. Since his fall, corruption in the oil industry resulting from the lack of differentiation includes the letting of contracts to service companies, a prerogative that has inappropriately but profitably been retained by the Ministry, rather than being devolved to the INOC and its component companies.[1]

The principal reason why adequate legal and administrative frameworks have yet to emerge is that overall policy for the oil industry has not been determined, which in turn reflects the fact that a functioning political system has yet to be constituted. The vital issues surrounding the reconstruction of the Iraqi oil industry, such as how it should be owned and operated and who should benefit from its revenues, are proxy questions for what the nature of Iraq's entire political economy is to be. As oil goes, so goes a nation where it provides more than 60 per cent of GDP and 95 per cent of both the government's revenues and hard currency earnings.[2] Since the fall of Saddam, various Iraqi political figures, including incumbent ministers of petroleum, have offered their views of appropriate futures for the oil industry.[3] The absence of an institutionalized political

1. According to one oil company executive, 'There is no fixed contract model, fixed tenders or schedules ...' He notes that bidding processes on tenders are 'somewhat opaque.' Boxell.

2. Ariel Cohen and Gerald P. O'Driscoll.

3. Former Minister of Oil Issam Chalabi claims that there was 'close to unanimity' that 'natural resources should remain under the sovereignty of the state.' Undersecretary of Oil Fadhil Chalabi is on record as endorsing the participation of foreign oil companies and partial privatization. See Duffield, p. 16. Former Prime Minister Ayad Allawi urged the newly elected parliament to allow foreign investment in the oil industry, noting that 'the state will no longer monopolise everything, including the oil

system, however, renders these views less than authoritative. So the Iraqi oil industry has operated in rudderless fashion, maintaining the flow of oil by dint of its own efforts, with assistance from the occupying powers, such as that provided by the US Army Corps of Engineers, and service companies. No major commitments for the upgrading of existing fields or facilities have yet been made, to say nothing of the lack of commitment as yet to developing new fields or further exploration. So the Iraqi oil industry, just like the country as a whole, is on the threshold of a new era, but even the broad outlines of that era remain obscure.

The new constitution drafted by the constitutional committee of the transitional parliament and passed by that body on 18 September 2005 and then ratified in a nationwide referendum on 15 October, has, if anything, rendered yet more confused the broad policy context within which the oil industry is to be developed. This confusion results in part from the compromise reached at the very last minute of the approval process, in which Sunnis were placated by a commitment to open up the constitution for reconsideration over a period of six months by the parliament to be elected on 15 December 2005.

---

sector, except for the upstream.' Cited in Khaled Yacoub Oweis, 'Iraq Parliament to Decide on Oil Rights,' Reuters, 19 January 2005. Finance Minister Abdel Mahdi told a gathering in Washington that he wants to see a new oil law that would open the national oil company to foreign investment and that foreigners would gain access even in upstream areas. See Antonia Juhasz, 'Of Oil and Elections,' Alternet, 27 January 2005. Thamir al Ghadban, Minister of Oil, welcomed 'Iraqi, Arab and foreign investments' in the oil sector, but ruled out privatization of 'the extraction sector.' *Oil and Gas Journal* Online, 16 and 28 February 2005. Ahmad Chalabi, according to the BBC Newsnight programme cited above, endorsed the wholesale privatization of Iraq's oil assets to international concerns.

Another cause of confusion was the actual articles pertaining to oil. Article 108 specifies that 'oil and gas are the ownership of all the people of Iraq *in all the regions and governorates.'* (emphasis added). This could be taken to mean that those living in areas of oil production are to have no special rights or claims. But Article 109 appears to suggest something else, as it calls for 'the damaged regions that were unjustly deprived by the former regime and the regions that were damaged later on' to receive 'a set allotment for a specified time' from existing production. These are oblique references to the Shi'a dominated South and the Kurdish controlled North of the country. Furthermore, the first and second clauses of Article 109 divide authority between the central government, on the one hand, and the provinces and regions, on the other. This latter category is an entirely new and highly controversial one, created by the constitution itself and giving any two provinces the right to band together to form a region, in which various powers would then be vested. With regard to oil, the powers that provinces and regions appear to have relate to the development of new fields, which is to be undertaken in an unspecified way with the federal government. Further complicating this already ambiguous picture is article 117, which assigns to 'regional authorities' all powers not reserved to the federal government; prioritizes regional over federal legislation 'in case of a contradiction;' and specifies that 'regions and governorates shall be allocated an equitable share of the national revenues sufficient to discharge their responsibilities and duties, but having regard to its resources, needs and the percentage of the population.'

Iraqi oil specialists are dismayed by these constitutional provisions because they fragment power over that industry in highly ambiguous fashion. One former Minister of Oil, Issam Chalabi, noted the key article 'looks like it was written by politicians with disregard to the complexity of such a policy that would definitely cause a lot of problems and disputes between the central government and the various regions and governorates and also among themselves.' He continued to note that 'it also restricts the role of the federal government in planning and managing the oil industry.'[1]

Given the precarious state of affairs in the country, it would be more than presumptuous for outsiders to expect Iraqis when reconstructing their oil industry to seek to apply best case, textbook models, whether neo-liberal or otherwise. Oil will be vital to the reconstruction of the country or possibly regions or even countries that emerge from what was a unified Iraq. It is the resource that can help bind the country together or contribute to it being torn apart. Its political importance, therefore, naturally takes precedence over all other matters.

At the same time, however, it is important that as many mistakes as possible be avoided during the reconstruction process, and that Iraqis be aware of the likely consequences of different policy choices. Decisions made now about the exploitation of the country's vast energy reserves may well profoundly impact the future. Whether through writing policies into a constitution or by enshrining them in other legal, economic and administrative arrangements, the Iraqis run the risk of foreclosing not only best, but also better case options for a long time to come, if not forever. There are many cases of overzealous resource nationalism having resulted in restrictive constitutional provisions that have seriously

---

1. Cited in *Middle East Economic Survey* (29 August 2005).

impeded the development of countries' hydrocarbon deposits, or which have led to the creation of natural resource funds that instead of providing economic stability or savings for future generations, have provided slush funds for ruling elites.[1] Similarly, misguided efforts to privatize hydrocarbon assets have led to vast and inappropriate transfers of assets from the public to private purses, with no commensurate gains in output or efficiency. So the choices Iraq makes now are of vital and likely lasting importance. While the pressure of circumstances renders effective decision-making problematical, every possible effort should be made to ensure that at least worst-case solutions are avoided. As much flexibility as possible should be maintained so that policies can be adjusted subsequently better to fit changed circumstances.

The two key questions that Iraqi policy makers have to answer with regard to their oil industry are who will own it and how are the revenues it generates to be allocated? With regard to the ownership question, the two basic alternative models are private versus public. The long history of public ownership in Iraq, the leading role that Baghdad played in the struggle by producing countries to gain control over their oil resources, the failure of neo-liberal reforms to sweep through Middle East oil industries, the urgent need to preserve the nation, and the lack of effective decision making and regulatory systems, all suggest that when the decision about ownership is made, it should and is likely to be toward the public, rather than private end of the continuum. Indeed, any decision for a dramatic privatization of the industry would be highly contentious and probably lack sufficient legitimacy to be fully or permanently

---

1.   On the propensity for this to occur and how to avoid it, see 'Protecting the Future: Constitutional Safeguards for Iraq's Oil Revenues,' *Revenue Watch*, report 8, (May 2005).

implemented. Even partial privatizations will come under careful scrutiny.[1]

But the matter does not rest there. The public-private dichotomy is less absolute and categorical than it once was or the terms imply. Moreover, the rhetoric of politicians, which seems to suggest a uniform, 'nationalist' approach, in reality camouflages differences. Iraqi decision makers themselves, for example, have staked out various positions along the public-private continuum, ranging from strong endorsements of continuation of the status quo of virtually complete public ownership, to varying degrees of privatization of downstream and possibly upstream operations, even to non-Iraqi purchasers.[2] But all discussions and pronouncements about this sensitive issue are cloaked with the rhetoric of strong national (or regional) public control over the resource, with even those advocating extensive privatization emphasizing the continuing commanding role of the state, either in its central or regional form, over private actors.[3]

---

1. According to Roger Diwan of PFC energy, 'privatization of the Iraqi oil sector is impractical – it would cause undue domestic political tension ... Maintaining the role of Iraq's national oil company is not inimical to good governance so long as the oil sector is independently regulated and contract bidding and award process is transparent.' He recommends that the Ministry of Oil regulate the sector, the INOC refurbish existing capacity, and foreign oil companies to develop new production as they have the technology and access to capital to do so. 'Iraqi Oil and the Iraqi State.' *A Special Presentation by PFC Energy*. DAC Meeting, Washington, D.C. (21–22 July 2003).

2. See note 3, pp. 18–19.

3. At a conference held in London in the summer of 2005 and attended by 'more than 60 Iraqi and international petroleum specialists, civil servants, policy makers, parliamentarians, activists, corporate executives, academics and journalists ... there was almost unanimous agreement that the oil sector should be led by a strong, commercially viable and independent national oil company.' 'Iraq Oil Wealth: Issues

In reality the prevailing models in most Third World producing countries, including virtually all of those in the Middle East, other than Iran, are those of Production Sharing Agreements (PSAs), which in reality are public-private partnerships, or service contracting by state owned companies with private national or international ones. Both models were utilized in Saddam's Iraq. In Iran, the contentious 'buy-back' model predominates, which is, in effect, also an agreement between the state and private oil companies, albeit on more rigid terms than are PSAs.[1] The real questions about public-private thus tend to be along a series of sub-continua, such as the terms, type and number of companies involved in PSAs; the degree to which the nationalized industry is 'unbundled', that is, functionally differentiated between policy making and implementation and within the latter, between and within upstream and downstream operations; the degree to which 'unbundled' components are commercialized and possibly privatized; the possible role of any lead IOC in the sector operating

---

of Governance and Development,' conference sponsored by the Open Society Institute and the London School of Economics (29 June – 1 July 2005), pp. 1, 10.

1.   The buy-back model became controversial during the June 2005 Iranian Presidential campaign. The reformist position was that the model was 'costly and damaging to oil reserves,' and had failed to attract foreign oil companies because of poor returns, whereas the Rafsanjani camp asserted that there were 'no specific problems with the buy-back system.' Numerous foreign companies, including Shell, have backed out of Iran because of dissatisfaction with the buy-back system, leaving only some six companies operating there. Partly as a result, the buy-back system has managed to add only about 500,000 barrels a day of output, about 12 per cent of total production, but barely ahead of the depletion rate. See Gareth Smyth and Kevin Morrison, 'Rafsanjani Rejects Oil Industry Reform,' *Financial Times* (9 June 2005), p. 9; and Carola Hoyos and Gareth Smyth, 'Iran's Officials Pledge Total Change to Oil Sector,' *Financial Times* (28 June 2005), p. 15.

under a PSA, in partnership with or possibly as co-owner with a local company; and so on. In sum, most oil industries are now mixed, public and private sector, national and international.[1] The rhetoric of politicians sometimes confuses this issue. So long as the rhetoric is not embedded in policies that prevent the natural evolution of ownership of oil industries as dictated by technical, economic, political, external and other factors, it probably is harmless. It may, in fact serve the useful purpose of ensuring public support. But the clear and present danger in Iraq is that today's political rhetoric might be concretized in policies and structures that cannot then be changed as the industry and the political economy evolve. This danger is further aggravated by the fact that policy preferences toward the ownership of the oil industry may be dictated more by narrow sectarian than broad national economic or political concerns, so that policy toward the oil industry is rational within the framework of sectarian politics, but irrational economically or in other terms.

The closely related and yet more contentious issue that Iraqi decision makers are presently grappling with is who should benefit from oil revenues? The rentier state constructed by Saddam, in which all revenues flowed to the government, is widely attributed as being a prime cause of its authoritarianism and failure adequately to develop other economic sectors. Moreover, increasing sectarianism and associated distrust – manifested in part by widespread suspicion that political and governmental institutions are the captives of this or that sect, tribe or other primordial grouping – naturally stimulate opposition to the idea that those national institutions should be the sole beneficiaries of oil revenues, rather than 'the people' themselves,

1. None, however, have voluntarily devolved ownership, as opposed to allocations of oil revenues, to sub-national levels

either individually or within region, sect or some other category. As a result, Iraq now confronts the danger of an over-reaction to the too centralized model of allocation of Saddam's rentier state. With the national state having under Saddam become dependent upon oil revenues for 95 per cent of its expenditures, it would be a Herculean task indeed to rapidly construct an effective state without it having a significant share of oil revenues, either directly or through taxation. Since the construction of an effective system of direct or indirect taxes would take some years, if the 'people', whether as individuals or in particular categories, become the immediate and direct beneficiaries of large portions of oil revenues, there is the twin danger of the state collapsing and of the oil industry lacking sufficient capital to maintain or upgrade its operations.[1]

While some Iraqis may in fact prefer that the state collapse, as some of those sceptical about the intentions of those who drafted the constitution suggest, at least public debate about the oil industry has not been predicated on this position. Instead, it has drawn upon alternative models extant in other countries where for the most part the possibly competitive interests of government – and different levels and regions of it – on the one hand, and individual citizens and groupings of them, on the other, have been successfully reconciled. Some of these models have attracted dedicated proponents, who see in them effective means of addressing political and economic problems. Probably the most messianic such model is that of direct payments to citizens, widely referred to as the 'Alaska model' and one openly endorsed by Ambassador Paul Bremer when he first arrived in Baghdad. Its potential benefits

---

1. According to one Iraqi expert, less than $1 billion of the $20 billion Iraq has been earning through oil exports 'returns to its domestic oil industry as investment.' Cited in 'Iraq Oil Wealth,' p. 5.

have also been sung by various US think tanks, including those on
the right as well as those dedicated to transparent and accountable
governance, and by some Iraqi organizations. The argument in
favour of the model is that by placing resources directly in the
hands of citizens, government will become their servant rather
than visa versa, a relationship from which various aspects of good
governance will flow, including transparency and accountability.[1]

While claims for other models have not been made in quite
such fulsome and all encompassing fashion, there are nevertheless
several which have support in particular Iraqi quarters and
which have proven viable in other settings. Various of these can
be grouped together under the general approach of devolving
revenues to non-national units of government, with those units
varying between regions, provinces or groupings of them, districts
and/or various local units. A standard practice elsewhere is for
resource producing regions to retain a share of revenues generated
from the extraction and sale of those resources, but the lack of
producing oil fields in Sunni-dominated regions of Iraq has made
this a problematical issue.[2] The novel approach adopted in the

---

1. Among those who have endorsed the allocation of oil earnings directly
   to citizens, typically by enshrining the principle in the constitution,
   are Michael E. O'Hanlon of the Brookings Institution ('A Sunni Role
   is Essential in New Iraq,' The Brookings Institution, Foreign Policy
   Studies, 18 January 2005); and Fawaz K. Saraf, 'Oil Dividend Paper,' The
   Iraq Foundation, 14 February 2005.

2. Some ways around this problem have, however, been suggested. David
   Phillips of the Council on Foreign Relations, for example, argues that
   'The New Iraq should be divided into five or six federal Iraqi states ...
   using geographic, not ethnic, criteria ... The national government should
   control Iraq's oil wealth and return a share to the regions based on
   population percentages ... While the (Sunni) region may lack oil, revenue
   sharing would assure them a portion of Iraq's energy wealth.' 'Iraq's Real
   Battle will be over Laws of the Land,' *Financial Times* (13 April 2005),

constitution is to differentiate between previously developed and new oil fields, allocating revenues from the former to regions and provinces without regard to their area of origin, but possibly reserving revenues to those areas in the case of reserves developed in the future. Whether what is essentially now a draft constitutional proposal remains in the final version and is then in fact applied, remains to be seen however.

Another model, which interestingly was virtually pioneered in Iraq under the monarchy in the form of the Development Board, is that of the Natural Resource Fund (NRF), which in its contemporary manifestations takes the form of a revenue stabilization fund, a savings device, or a loan fund for specified types of undertakings, such as development or welfare. Finally, a related approach is to focus not only on the beneficiaries of oil revenues, but also on the use of those revenues to leverage reform of political and economic governance. Most notable in this regard are proposals to adopt constitutional provisions that specify not only who should receive revenues, but how they should be managed, with the hope that this will improve the quality of revenue management more generally, especially its transparency. By vesting the power to manage these revenues in elected bodies, most notably the national parliament, advocates of this approach hope thereby to support democratization as well as good governance.[1]

---

p. 19. Iraq Revenue Watch of the Open Society Institute argues that the constitution should explicitly include oil income and expenditure in the budgetary process and should 'ensure that both the national government and the provincial and/or local governments have a role in petroleum exploration and development, and in deciding how to spend the resulting revenues.' 'Constitutional Safeguards for Iraq's Oil Revenues: Key to Future Stability,' www.iraqrevenuewatch.org/reports/052605.shtml

1.   See for example Paul Davies and Peter Young, 'Towards an Economic

Iraq is thus simultaneously confronting not only the two key questions surrounding resource extraction in Third World countries, but doing so as it is seeking to save the nation and build a new state. As if that were not enough, it is doing so while the global energy system is becoming more controversial as it assumes steadily more importance for the world economy. While there is a growing diversity of models of ownership and allocation in Third World producing countries, these national energy sectors nevertheless remain comparatively resistant to neo-liberal orthodoxies. The hopes that Iraq might both resolve the present energy crisis and break the logjam holding up neo-liberal reforms, apparently entertained by American neo-conservatives, clearly are not going to be realized in the near future.

But that does not preclude the possibilities that decisions made by Iraqis about their oil industry now will in a few years significantly impact global energy markets and the organization of national energy sectors. With more than 10 per cent of the world's proven oil reserves, stagnant and even declining oil production, and an economy that is failing even to sustain standards of living or reduce record unemployment, it is clear that there are profound internal and external pressures on Iraq to attempt to rapidly redevelop its oil industry. Reconciling the need for as rapid a recovery of production as possible and the yet more profound need of preserving the nation, with the need to lay the foundations for long-term growth of the oil industry and the country as a whole, is a major challenge.

In order better to meet this challenge, Iraqi decision makers need access to as much information as possible about comparative

_____

and Governance Agenda for a New Iraq,' Adam Smith Institute, London (March 2003).

experiences and possible approaches that they might adopt. Numerous efforts have been made to this end, including those by governments, think tanks, IOCs and others. The study that follows is a revised version of one such example. It was originally commissioned in the spring of 2003 by the UK Department for International Development (DFID), to feed into decision-making processes in Baghdad about the future of the Iraqi oil industry and its relationship to the political economy more broadly. Because authoritative decisions about the reconstruction of the oil industry and the political economy more generally have not yet been completed, despite references to it in what remains de facto a provisional constitution, and because the decision making system and those within it have changed since the paper was first produced, it seems appropriate for it to be reissued and to reach a wider audience. This has necessitated some updating, but surprisingly and in fact disturbingly little, given the vital importance of the Iraqi oil industry, both nationally and internationally. The original paper was the product of all the authors, while this new introduction and revisions are principally the work of the lead author.

The paper asks two key questions of alternative models for the Iraqi oil industry – who will own it and how will the revenues it generates be allocated? Theoretically possible answers to both queries are organized into four-celled tables defined by the dimensions *centralized – decentralized* and *public – private*. The possible models are then subjected to evaluation, the criteria for which include the impact of the model on the balance, both political and economic, between the state and non-state actors (including civil society) and between the governmental centre and periphery. Other primarily political criteria are whether the model would contribute to politically centrifugal or centripetal forces; would support or undermine legal/regulatory institutions and processes; and would facilitate or undermine the coherence of national policy making for the hydrocarbon sector. Economic criteria include whether or not the ownership model would provide access to capital and technology; would contribute to an effective balance between public and private sectors; would stimulate growth of other economic sectors; and could be implemented within a reasonable time frame. Lastly, the potential social impacts of alternative models are briefly evaluated in terms of their differential consequences for particular population groups, defined by both horizontal (i.e., relative wealth) and vertical (i.e., ethno-religious) cleavages.

It is hoped that this somewhat mechanistic, even antiseptic approach to what are intensely vital political and economic issues, renders their understanding and analysis somewhat more rational and balanced than they might otherwise be. The intended audience, moreover, is not just those involved in making decisions for Iraq. Indeed, what is surprising in the literature emanating from think tanks, other organizations and individual scholars is the degree to which it appears to be partisan, endorsing and advocating a particular approach and typically ignoring others, to say nothing of overlooking weaknesses of the one advocated. Moreover, other assessments typically are only partial, looking at ownership or allocation alone, or some aspect of them, rather than the totality of the Iraqi oil sector and its relationship to the broader political economy. So this effort is intended to be both reasonably comprehensive within the space available, and non-partisan. It is the case, however, that a special effort has been made to more carefully scrutinize solutions that appear in the first instance to be most persuasive, if only to try to ensure that they are carefully considered before being endorsed or adopted by whatever audiences. Similarly, because the available literature does not appear to place much emphasis on contemporary oil industries and their operational requirements, an effort has been made to pay special attention to the impact of policies on the Iraqi oil industry, if only to suggest that some policies can injure if not kill the goose that lays the golden egg.

The authors would like to thank Ms Anna Wilde of the Department for International Development (DFID) for agreeing to the publication of the amended version of the original study, and for her guidance and assistance in the preparation of that study. They would also like to thank Charles Buderi and David Nagel for their comments on it.

The Challenge

Oil-dependent economies, whether in the developed or developing world, are typically exposed to 'Dutch disease', whereby oil driven currency appreciation undermines competitiveness of tradable goods, reinforcing the oil-dependence and over-urbanisation of those economies.[1] Developing oil rich countries also typically suffer the political disease of authoritarianism. Oil revenues accrue directly to these 'rentier' states, obviating their need to extract resources from citizens, hence to be accountable to them. This logic of 'no taxation, no representation,' although no doubt an

---

1. Literature on the 'Dutch disease' is voluminous, some of which suggests that its impact may be less on poorer, labour abundant countries than first thought. See for example Alan Gelb, *Oil Windfalls: Blessing or Curse?* New York: Oxford University Press, 1988; and Michael L. Ross, 'The Political Economy of the Resource Curse,' *World Politics* 51, 2 (January 1999), 297–322. But the observation of a recent World Bank study, namely, 'very few developing or transitional economies with a rich petroleum endowment have become success stories in development and poverty elimination,' suggests, as that study concludes, that 'oil wealth is more often a curse than a blessing.' See Philip Daniel, 'Petroleum Revenue Management: An Overview,' study prepared for the World Bank, ESMAP Programme, no date.

oversimplified explanation of authoritarianism, does accord with the empirical reality of rentier states in the Middle East and North Africa (MENA) in general and Iraq in particular.[1]

The correlation between the Ba'thist state's increasing economic autonomy over its thirty-five year life with its growing political despotism is suggestive. The state owned and controlled oil industry accounted for approximately twice as much of the GDP in 2003 than in 1989.[2] By the mid 1990s non-oil Iraqi exports withered to some one per cent of the total. At the end of Saddam's regime the state had come to directly control over 80 per cent of the economy and employed at least 1.2 million individuals and paid pensions to another 350,000, making some two in five Iraqi households directly dependent on the government for their primary means of support, to say nothing of the almost total dependence of the entire population on the state's food rationing system established under the UN-mandated oil-for-food programme.[3] Taxation, never a preponderant source of state revenue, has all but disappeared as one. Writing recently, a political economist who brought the term 'rentier state' into vogue more than two decades ago, stated that while oil revenues brought about a 'remarkable improvement of essential government services' in Iraq, 'the vast resources put into the hands of the central government strengthened it against

1. A classic theoretical statement of the rentier state argument as applied to the MENA is Hazem Biblawi, 'The Rentier State in the Arab World,' in Giacomo Luciani, ed., *The Arab State*. Berkeley: University of California Press, 1990. A recent empirical study suggests confirmation of the argument. See Michael L. Ross, 'Does Oil Hinder Democracy?' *World Politics* 53, 3 (April 2001), 325–361.

2. Richard Murphy, 'Winning the Peace: Managing a Successful Transition in Iraq.' Washington, D.C.: American University and the Atlantic Council (January 2003), p. 7.

3. *Ibid.*, pp. 6–7.

competing power centres in society.' Having access to oil revenues 'relieved the government from the necessity of extracting resources from society' and the need to offer participation in decision-making. Those same revenues underpinned investments 'in political patronage and the security apparatus, making any challenge to the ruling coalition extremely difficult.'[1]

Paradoxically, although the Iraqi economy and the ruling Ba'thists were extremely dependent on the oil industry, comparatively little was done to develop it. Possibly the most revealing indicator of this retarded development is that Iraq has drilled only some 2,000 oil wells, compared to about one million in Texas. Of its seventy-three known fields, only fifteen have been exploited.[2] Iraq possesses the world's second largest proven oil reserves, which may be considerably larger than the official figure of 112 billion barrels. Production costs of about $2 per barrel are among the lowest in the world.[3] Iraq's average production over the past twenty-five years has been in the 2–3 million barrels per day range, a level that places it on a par with countries which have significantly lower reserves and behind the world's leading producers which, other than Saudi Arabia, have smaller reserves than Iraq. Gas reserves of some 110 trillion cubic feet are virtually totally unexploited. After thirteen years of sanctions and minimal investment in existing fields, to say nothing of wartime destruction and subsequent looting and sabotage, Iraq's production is now struggling to maintain half of nominal capacity.

---

1. Giacomo Luciani and Felix Neugart, 'Toward a European Strategy for Iraq,' EUI Policy Paper, (March 2003), pp. 6–7.

2. US Department of Energy, www.eia.doe.gov/emeu/cabs/orevcoun. html#Iraq. Iraqi Oil Minister, Amir Rashid, stated in 2002 that twenty-four fields had been exploited.

3. John Roberts, 'Oil and the Iraq War of 2003,' unpublished paper, Edinburgh, Methinks Ltd., p. 3.

The challenge then is to draw upon Iraq's vast and relatively under exploited oil reserves to rebuild the country, but to do so in a way that avoids the twin perils of 'Dutch disease' in the economy and authoritarianism in the polity. This challenge is rendered yet more formidable by the urgent need for restoration of basic services, which dictates all due haste for the revitalization of the oil industry in order to pay for those services; coupled with the possibly contradictory need not to make decisions that prematurely foreclose options or violate the fundamental principle that it is Iraqis and their duly constituted government who must decide how their national patrimony of oil is to be owned and developed. This principle is not just one of international political morality or of 'good politics.' It is enshrined in the Geneva Convention of 1949 and explicitly for the US in a 1976 Memorandum of Law, which states 'international law does not support the assertion of a right in the occupant to grant an oil development concession.'[1]

It should also be noted that the future of the Iraqi oil industry is of vital importance not just to Iraq's immediate oil producing neighbours, including Iran, Kuwait and Saudi Arabia, but also to the world energy system as a whole. As regards Middle Eastern producers, their declining share of global oil exports is due in part to their reluctance to adopt neo-liberal reforms that would presumably lift production. If Iraq were to do so, it might cause Gulf and other MENA producers to follow suit, thus bringing about significant changes in world oil supplies and their control, to say nothing of repercussions for OPEC. The stakes are obviously high and the external pressures upon Iraq are weighty and numerous. This makes it all the more important for Iraqis to

---

1. *Ibid*, p. 8.

have an accurate understanding of the domestic economic and political consequences that will result from the way in which their oil industry is rebuilt. The emergence of a viable, effective and lasting national consensus on this vital issue will depend on that understanding. Failure to achieve consensus will increase the likelihood that external pressures and interests will assume greater, possibly decisive importance, probably to the detriment of Iraq.

Allocation

Those who own the oil industry may not be the same as those who receive allocations directly or indirectly from it. Privately owned oil companies, for example, pay dividends to their (share)owners and taxes to public authorities. In some cases such companies may also be compelled by constitutional provisions to make allocations to specific beneficiaries, such as in Alaska where at least one quarter of oil royalty revenues are paid into the Alaska Permanent Fund, which, among other activities, distributes annual cash payments to citizens of that state. In other settings some taxes on oil companies are earmarked for specific purposes, such as in Texas, where they are dedicated to the state university. The profits of state-owned oil companies may accrue to the state's general revenues, or may be earmarked in part or in whole for specific purposes. In Kuwait, for example, a percentage of the earnings of the national oil company have been paid into a special fund, which has invested those revenues, nominally on behalf of subsequent generations.

Because ownership of component companies of an oil industry is less than a perfect guide to who receives direct resource allocations from them, it seems appropriate to look at ownership and allocation separately before briefly speculating on possible combinations of them. By combining different models of ownership and allocation, it may be possible to satisfy multiple objectives and/or constituencies. Privatization of ownership, for example, coupled with preferential allocations via royalties, earmarked taxes or other levies, might simultaneously accomplish efficiency and welfare objectives, while paving the way for political acceptance. Indeed, the former head of the Coalition Provisional Authority, Paul Bremer, in his statement in the June 2003 World Economic Forum in Amman, intimated that such earmarking of revenues combined with privatization was his preferred model for the oil industry.

Allocations can be to public instrumentalities or to private organizations or individuals and they can be made at the centralized, national level or in a decentralized fashion. The two axes of public – private and centralized – decentralized, thus create a four-fold table as follows:

Allocation

	Public	Private
Centralized	Natural (non-renewable) resource funds; social safety nets	National trust with investments/loans to private companies
Decentralized	Revenue sharing with provincial/local governments	Pension or other direct payment scheme

Public Centralized Allocations

Allocations of earnings from the oil industry to centralized, autonomous public bodies, generally now known as Natural Resource Funds (NRFs), can be for the purpose of stabilizing oil earnings over time, providing savings for the future, or for other specified purposes, typically of a developmental or welfare nature. Whatever their purpose, the implied rationale is that the exigencies of politics and government are such that competing demands for the revenues are likely to take precedence if those resources are not walled off from typical expenditure procedures, such as inclusion in state budgets. An increasingly common way of establishing and guaranteeing the continued existence of NRFs is to enshrine them in constitutions. In general the critique of NRFs is not of their intended purpose, but of their unintended side effects or of their mismanagement. The typical rejoinder to these criticisms is that shortcomings can be overcome through better constitutional and institutional safeguards, begging the question as to whether or not this in turn is possible in poorly institutionalized political systems.[1]

Two proximate examples of NRFs – the Kuwaiti Fund for the Future and the former Iraqi Development Board – illustrate the problems of corruption/mismanagement and unintended, negative consequences developing over time. The Kuwaiti Fund for the Future, created at independence, was intended, as the name implies, to be a sinking fund to offset depletion of oil reserves. Its operations, like many of the activities of the Kuwait Petroleum Corporation, which generated the profits from which the Fund was financed, were not included in the state budget, hence subject

---

1. See for example 'Protecting the Future.'

to parliamentary oversight. Some twenty years after its creation the Fund became mired in scandal when it was revealed that losses had been incurred as a result of unsound investments, which in turn seemed to have been made as a result of kickbacks provided to its managers, in turn protected by members of the ruling family. The paradox is that had these oil revenues been treated as a normal component of the state budget, rather than as a NRF, they would have been subject to the scrutiny of the comparatively active and powerful Kuwaiti parliament.

Subjecting the Kuwaiti Fund to parliament's oversight is one obvious solution to this problem, but that approach would not solve the related problem of the poor performance of the Fund and the Kuwait Petroleum Corporation in comparison to that of most IOCs and indeed many other national oil companies. Had the latter been effectively commercialized and internationalized, there is every likelihood it would have increased its net annual earnings many times over what in fact they are. The argument that the future generations of Kuwaitis would be protected by virtue of the existence of the Fund may have militated against pressure to ensure that the producer of Kuwait's wealth – its national oil company – be managed in such a way as to ensure maximum possible returns. This possible unintended consequence has, along with the poor and indeed criminal management of the fund itself, substantially reduced the net wealth of the country.

Adequate oversight was also not achieved in the case of the Iraqi Development Board, although in this case the problem was less that of corruption than inappropriate utilization of resources. Set up to invest a fixed percentage of earnings from the Iraqi oil industry in capital development projects, the Board favoured capital rather than labour intensive projects and totally ignored the housing sector, failing thereby to alleviate unemployment and poverty, chief causes of the revolution that overthrew the monarchy.

In the cases of both the Fund and the Board, the desire to make them essentially autonomous contributed both to financial impropriety and to preventing them from being used as instruments of government policy. In their desire to place the Fund and the Board 'above politics,' those who designed them denied governments an important potential tool for economic management. Moreover, because they were isolated from the state's normal administrative apparatus, their operations could not contribute to the development of the public administration. Indeed, they may have served as a disincentive for the state to undertake civil service reforms.

The most obvious potential liability of allocating earnings from the oil industry to centralized, autonomous public bodies, is the lack of adequate oversight, but that is by no means the only possible shortcoming. Unintended negative consequences on the political economy more generally, such as exerting a drag effect on reform, also result from the creation and operation of NRFs. Such funds may deprive governments of resources that can be used for short-term economic management as well as long-term development of the state's administrative capacities. Moreover, by placing such bodies 'above politics,' their very existence casts doubts on the integrity and competence of the political system generally and the government in particular. Finally, predetermined allocations to such bodies preclude flexible approaches by economic and political decision makers, who may rightly assess some time in the future that the balance between capital and recurrent budgetary expenditures, for example, is inappropriate, but can do nothing to correct that balance.[1]

In sum, earmarkings of oil derived revenues to autonomous or quasi-autonomous public bodies charged with performing a particular function might be appropriate in particular circumstances, such as when government is extremely weak and the political system highly fragmented, or when that government is very powerful but has a long tradition of lack of accountability. When these conditions prevail the inability of government to spend the largesse wisely, combined with the possibility that the struggle for oil revenues will further fragment an already divided body politic, may suggest that at least for a temporary period the potential costs of this type of earmarking may be less than the likely costs of other ways of allocating revenues.

---

1. Since 1960, thirteen Nonrenewable Resource Funds have been established in countries ranging from Chile to Venezuela to Norway and even the United States (Alaska). Those in Oman and Papua New Guinea palpably failed and were abolished. Those of Azerbaijan and Iran are typical of such Funds. Established by Presidential Decree, the Azerbaijan fund had accumulated $630 million from state profit shares of oil sales by September 2002. Its primary purposes are to serve as a 'rainy day' hedge against future economic uncertainties, and to provide for capital developments, such as an oil pipeline. Parliament has no control over expenditures from the fund, which is directly under the President. Established more than two years ago, the Iranian Oil Stabilisation Fund receives revenues earned over and above the government's budgeted price estimate and had accumulated some $1 billion by January 2001. Half of these resources can be drawn upon when and if world prices drop below the government's budgeted level and the other half is reserved to develop exports and the private sector. Its operations are not transparent and it is widely rumoured that its resources have been drawn upon for other purposes. Other countries, including Algeria and Trinidad and Tobago, have established stabilization funds, the sole purpose of which is to iron out the economic consequences of fluctuations in oil prices.

But it is precisely in such circumstances that effective oversight even of constitutionally established and protected NRFs is most difficult to accomplish. Recommendations to subject such funds to oversight by parliament are of little avail when parliament itself is effectively subordinate to the executive, as the cases of Nigeria, Indonesia, Chad and elsewhere suggest. Moreover, because the creation of NRFs deprives the political system of a resource that could be vital for its development, it is likely to prolong the very conditions it is intended to avoid. For that reason these types of earmarkings should probably be limited in time, function, and magnitude of resources. When such earmarkings are made they should be explicitly stated to be of a transitional nature, with appropriate criteria established to indicate when the roles of the relevant autonomous body or bodies should be reduced or abolished. In that way incentives would be provided for political and economic actors to achieve certain developmental objectives, such as the holding of free and fair elections, establishment of an autonomous central bank, creation of effective regulatory structures, etc. A recent World Bank study concluded that a Natural Resource Fund 'is no substitute for sound overall fiscal and economic management but in certain circumstances it may buttress the right policy mix.'[1]

Allocations to non-autonomous instrumentalities of central government are of course also possible. The analogy to so-called sin taxes on tobacco and alcohol, a portion of which are sometimes earmarked for public health systems, exemplifies how such a

---

1. Daniel, p. 34. A recent critical study of the efficacy of these funds is James A. Daniel, 'Hedging Government Oil Price Risk,' IMF Working Paper, Fiscal Affairs Department, WP/01/185, November 2001.

Social Funds and Poverty Alleviation Programmes in the MENA Region

The main social funds are the Algerian Social Development Agency, the Egyptian Social Fund for Development (SFD), the Yemeni SFD and the West Bank and Gaza Community Development and NGO programmes. The importance of social funds in the overall social protection system and for job creation varies from one country to another: The SFD is of moderate importance in Egypt, while in Algeria it has had only a negligible impact. Egypt's SFD has assisted some 63,000 small businesses, with loans averaging $5,000; and its community development programme has assisted more than 40,000 micro-entrepreneurs with loans averaging $500. The percentage of Egyptians living in poverty, however, has risen steadily during the years in which the SFD has operated. It has frequently been the target of criticisms, including allegations about excessive remunerations to staff and to politicians.

In Morocco and Tunisia there are direct transfer programmes. Morocco's Entraide Nationale (EN) is a public establishment under the authority of Morocco's Ministry of Social Development and Social Solidarity. Its mission has been to support the poor. But of an estimated 5-6 million poor, EN reaches only 80,000 (1.6 per cent of the poor). In Tunisia the Ministry of Social Affairs provides direct transfer programmes to the hardcore poor. Although the number of households benefiting from direct cash transfers has been increasing, coverage is still inadequate, including the poorest areas in the northwest and centre-west. In both these programmes administration is complex, requiring large numbers of employees.

system could operate.[1] Paul Bremer was quoted as referring to the need for oil revenues to be used in part to create a social safety net, implying that this measure should accompany privatization of the oil industry. Presumably that social safety net would be operated by the central government, possibly through line ministries such as those for health, education or employment, or conceivably through an equivalent to the Social Funds established by the World Bank. These Social Funds typically report directly to cabinets or prime ministers and enjoy some, but not a great deal of autonomy from government. That they have generally not lived up to expectations may indicate a fundamental shortcoming of this centralized administrative approach to creating a social safety net, or it may imply that conditions characteristic of low and even middle income developing economies are inimical to the very concept of a social safety net, which may be viable only in more developed economies (see box).

Whatever the case regarding the social welfare consequences of earmarking oil revenues for activities authorized and possibly conducted directly by the central government, this approach has advantages and disadvantages for the political economy. Among the former are that such expenditures may buy loyalty to and support for the political system; they may contribute to improving human resource capacities; they may provide indirect resources for civil society by relieving individuals and families from expenditure burdens for basic services, thus freeing up their resources for other expenditures, some of which may assist private

---

1. The Norwegian State Petroleum Fund has some of the characteristics of this approach. Accountable to the legislature and integrated into the state's budgetary process, it is intended primarily to generate long-term savings to counteract the economic effects of an ageing population.

voluntary associations or other organizations of civil society; and the management/delivery of human services may assist in the development of broader governmental capacities. If this approach were explicitly combined with a reduction in public employment as part of a reform of the civil service, so that welfare and employment were clearly separated (which is not the case at present in Iraq and many other Arab countries), by facilitating that reform it could make a major contribution to improving governance and ultimately, economic performance.[1]

The disadvantages for the political economy of allocating specific portions of oil revenues to centralized public instrumentalities, especially those responsible for health, education and welfare services, are as follows:

1. Reinforcing actual and perceived linkages between oil

---

1. The case of Chad could provide some lessons for Iraq. In 1998 its parliament passed a revenue management law that is designed to ensure that earnings from oil are directed to poverty reduction. Under the law, 10 per cent of the royalties and dividends will be held in trust for future generations, while 80 per cent of the remaining funds will be devoted to education, health and social services, rural development, infrastructure, and environmental and water resource management. 5 per cent will be earmarked for regional development in the oil-producing area (over and above its share of national spending). In addition, the law created an oversight committee (Petroleum Revenues Oversight Committee) to monitor the use of the oil revenues. This committee of nine members includes representatives of the Government, Parliament, the judiciary, and civil society. A related programme is supporting the work of the oversight committee, as well as strengthening Chad's general accounting office and the dissemination of information about government expenditures. Despite all of these safeguards, the World Bank in August 2005, expressed 'serious concern' about the use being made by the government of oil revenues. See Dino Mahtani, 'World Bank Concern over Chad Oil Revenues,' *Financial Times* (20 August 2005).

revenue and centralized public service delivery, may create resistance to subsequent policy changes (e.g., privatization/ decentralization of the oil industry and of welfare services);

2. It may militate against development of public – private linkages in these sectors and in the economy more broadly, while reducing incentives to create appropriate regulatory systems;

3. Accountability and transparency (to say nothing of efficiency and cost effectiveness) may be particularly difficult to establish when large expenditures of resources are mandated by law, especially when those expenditures are for public welfare purposes;

4. Finally, and most importantly, resources allocated to centralized, public instrumentalities could serve as patronage for politicians and administrators in positions to direct the flow of those resources. The oil-for-food programme, used as a means of political control by Saddam's regime, illustrates how such a system, when taken to extremes, can become the very backbone of control by an authoritarian government.[1]

In sum, there are major potential political and economic disadvantages in allocating oil revenues to either autonomous or non-autonomous, centralized public instrumentalities, even (and maybe especially if) they are utilized for health, education and welfare services. While such systems may win political support for the government and contribute to the improvement

---

1. Daniel concludes his assessment of petroleum revenue distribution for the World Bank by stating that 'extra-budgetary funds ... carry significant disadvantages ... It will usually be preferable to put the general budgeting system right rather than to use extra-budgetary funds.' p. 44.

of human well-being and capacities, they might only do so at the costs of precluding subsequent alternatives and of rendering democratization less likely. Bismarckian welfare, for example, did not democratize Prussia, it reinforced authoritarianism. Moreover, by placing major issues of public allocations beyond the reach of normal political decision-making, politics and the institutions within which they occur, such as the parliament, are implicitly trivialized. A major economic downside is that efficiency incentives are all but eliminated, including those for innovation in service delivery. At most, then, if such systems are adopted it should be for a fixed and phased transitional period, although this approach is a risky one, for structures of entitlement immediately create their own constituencies.

Public Decentralized Allocations

It is possible to allocate oil revenues to non-national units of government for specific purposes or for general budgetary support. The latter approach is in fact embodied, albeit in vague terms, in the draft of the Iraqi constitution ratified in October 2005. It is also an approach advocated in a prominent European – American policy paper released just at the time of the invasion.[1] The authors observed that 'power in Iraq should be dispersed, thereby creating a system of checks and balances that prevents the re-establishment of a strong, centralized authoritarian rule ... The establishment of an inclusive and accountable political system in Iraq requires the distribution of the oil rent among several centres of power (possibly

---

1. Giacomo Luciani and Fleix Neugart, 'Toward a European Strategy for Iraq,' Florence, European University Institute, in cooperation with the Aspen Institute, The Royal Institute of International Affairs, and the Bertelsmann Foundation, March 2003, pp. 7, 11.

federal entities).' In other words, both international supporters of general principles of democratic governance, and incumbent Iraqi political elites who have to wrestle with the increasingly sectarian demands of their fellow citizens, concur in the wisdom of decentralizing allocations.

The initial US-supported effort to rebuild the Iraqi political system incorporated a revenue decentralization programme as part of a United States Agency for International Development (USAID) led activity to revitalize and democratize provincial and local level government.[1] Throughout the Arab world the lack of democratic and effective units of government below the national level remains a serious obstacle to democratization and improved governance. A 'democratization from the bottom up' strategy, which would start by concentrating on local and/or provincial governments, had it succeeded in Iraq, could have presaged a major breakthrough for the region more generally. In the event, the USAID effort was abandoned in November 2003 when the CPA, under orders from the White House, decided on a rapid transfer of power through national elections. But the questions remain as to whether some type of revenue sharing programme that would benefit sub-national levels of government would reinforce or impede both their democratization and that of Iraq as a whole, and whether it would retain or undermine the unity of the country. These questions are so vital precisely because decentralized allocations are provided for

---

1. A strong recommendation for decentralization is contained in a report commissioned by Secretary of Defense Donald Rumsfeld and Paul Bremer. That report states that 'decentralization is essential,' and that 'the CPA should provide local and provincial councils with funds to address priority local infrastructure needs.' John Hamre, et. al., 'Iraq's Post-Conflict Reconstruction.' Washington, D.C.: Centre for Strategic and International Studies (July 2003), ii, 4.

by the constitution formally now in effect.

On the positive side, a revenue sharing programme could help counterbalance national government, thereby contributing to pluralism. Political participation would 'follow the Dinar,' leading citizens, civil society organizations and political parties to concentrate more of their attention at local/provincial levels. Intensified political competition at this level could provide opportunities for more Iraqis to engage in politics in a peaceful, democratic contest to decide who gets what, when and how. That contest might contribute to blurring the lines of sectarian division, at least in those areas with mixed populations. Local and provincial governments would thus not only counterbalance the centre, they would provide aspiring politicians with learning opportunities and ultimately channels of recruitment to the national level. In an effort to promote the realization of this happy scenario, a revenue sharing programme could include performance benchmarks against which local/provincial units of government could be evaluated, with those evaluations playing some role in determining actual revenue allocations.[1]

An elaborate, benchmark-based revenue sharing programme would be ambitious given the present circumstances of an Iraq increasingly divided along sectarian lines, but some benefits might flow from even a very simplified approach, such as at least recognizing principles of good governance as a basis for reward

---

1. It is unrealistic, however, in light of Iraq's present economic and administrative circumstances, to seek in the next couple of years to establish an effective system of personal income tax. Moreover, establishing formulae for revenue sharing would have to take account of distortions introduced by the previous, highly centralized system and of the desire to induce decentralizations, including that of population redistribution.

through allocation. Revenue sharing could be utilized to enhance equity between regions, possibly thereby reinforcing centripetal forces in the country as a whole. Revenue sharing that would benefit the relatively poor, primarily agricultural dependent Shiʿa areas of the South, for example, could be used as an incentive to maintain Shiʿa support for the nation of Iraq. Revenue sharing could also enable local and provincial governments to innovate in various ways, including methods of service delivery. A healthy competition between provinces to improve services for their citizens and to attract investments could be of benefit to all and would set an example for the rest of the Arab world.

But significant potential liabilities are also associated with allocating oil revenues to non-national units of government. Most importantly, this approach could exacerbate centrifugal political forces, undermining national unity and cohesion while reinforcing geographically based ethnic, religious, tribal, or other loyalties. Because the primary oil producing areas are the Kurdish dominated North and the Shiʿa dominated South, allocations based only and strictly on geographic principles would exacerbate rather than ameliorate inter-communal tensions. This would especially be the case were the allocations made on regional (i.e., North, South, Centre) as opposed to provincial (i.e., governorate) bases. Even in the case of the latter, however, the fact that the principle of federalism, now incorporated into the constitution, will permit provinces to join together into regions, will render such an approach even more politically sensitive. It is also the case that strengthening provincial and local at the expense of national government could provide institutional bases for political leaders promoting the particularistic agendas of Kurds, Shiʿites, or others. Possibilities that such particularistic interests, including tribes or religious organizations, could capture local or provincial governments are higher than they are at the more heterogeneous, politically more competitive centre. Once local or provincial 'commanding heights' were conquered, those in control, reinforced by patronage resources from the centre, could be very hard to dislodge.

Instead of reducing tendencies toward authoritarianism resulting from a rentier economy, allocating revenues to provincial or local governments might simply reproduce 'rentierism' in those settings. Provincial and local elites could be tempted to convert guaranteed revenues (rents) flowing from the centre into resources for patronage. Presumably this conversion would be much more difficult if those elites were forced to raise resources locally, in which case citizens would have more incentive to hold their public officials accountable. At a minimum, allocations from the governmental centre to the periphery would do nothing to encourage fiscal responsibility, for competition would focus on obtaining more of the 'free' resources from that centre, rather than on enhancing local efficiencies and economies. Revenue sharing could discourage efforts at local revenue raising, further devaluing political needs for accountability and transparency. From the practical perspective of need for urgency, it might well be easier to establish a functioning government and administration in the centre rather than working to do so in an undetermined number of regions, eighteen provinces and scores of cities and towns. Moreover, the resource requirements of the central government for reconstructing national infrastructure, let alone for investment in development projects, will for the foreseeable future exceed resources made available by the oil industry. Sharing revenues with lower levels of government might actually delay national reconstruction unless those revenues were managed in an effective and coordinated fashion, tall orders given their complete lack of relevant previous experience and authority.[1]

As for the social impact of this model, international experience in fiscal decentralization in Africa and Asia points to limited success in achieving poverty alleviation and other social objectives. The reasons for this include: (i) lack of administrative and technical expertise at the local levels has meant that functions in sectors such as health and education were decentralized to levels which had no experience in implementing them; (ii) local parliaments are either unable to control corrupt local politicians or are complicit in their behaviour; and (iii) poor revenue mobilization at the local level leads to macroeconomic instability due to excessive borrowing and deficit financing for local budgets. Lessons from relatively more successful decentralization cases point to the necessity of ensuring sub-national policy-making autonomy and need for clarity in the roles and responsibilities between the central and the local governments. Appendix A provides some comparative examples of attempts to decentralize and lessons learned from them. It is worth noting the presence of oil revenues seems at least in some cases to complicate rather than smooth the process of decentralization.

Despite these potential liabilities, political pressures may require that some percentage of revenues be assigned directly on a geographic basis. Other countries in not altogether dissimilar circumstances have done so, typically assigning those revenues to the areas of actual oil production. Nigeria, for example, earmarks

---

1. This in fact was a fear expressed by many Iraqis present at the June-July London conference sponsored by the Open Society Institute and the London School of Economics.

13 per cent of oil revenues to the region of origin, whereas Chad assigns 5 per cent. Papua New Guinea gives all royalties to the provinces where oil is extracted, of which a portion is handed over directly to those who own the land where the oil is extracted. As this sample suggests, however, this method is by no means foolproof in overcoming hostility toward the central government. Whether it has ameliorated some dissatisfaction, or has stoked desires for further separation from the centre, is not clear. A recent study cautions that effective decentralization of allocations requires the systematic elaboration of programs, structures, plans and formal agreements that tie local governmental units to the centre.[1] This is a requirement that Iraq will not be able to meet for the foreseeable future. Nigeria, a country that has had some form of federal revenue sharing since colonial times in an attempt to 'placate separatist tendencies', has neither accomplished that objective nor has it managed to create the institutional framework that would in turn enable it to achieve other objectives, such as improved equity between regions. Although a recent study holds out hope that in Nigeria a 'properly designed federal transfer system can work ... ', that this observation is based on theoretical observations and that reality remains so much at variance, should certainly give pause to those hoping to accomplish something similar in Iraq.[2]

Iraq's current social conditions and factors related to them should be taken into account in the design of any public allocation of funds, whether centralized or decentralized. The especially

---

1. Allen L. Clark and Jennifer Cook Clark, 'The New Reality of Mineral Development: Social and Cultural Issues in Asia and Pacific Nations,' *Reesources Policy*, 25, 3 (1999), cited in Daniel, p. 46.

2. Ehtisham Ahmad and Raju Singh, 'Political Economy of Oil-Revenue Sharing in a Developing Country: Illustrations from Nigeria,' IMF Working Paper WP/03/16.

salient aspects of those conditions and key factors related to them include:

1) The poor: Income inequality in real terms grew especially rapidly after 1996, as wealth was concentrated increasingly in the hands of regime supporters. Demand and output presently are at historic lows. GDP per capita is currently estimated by the World Bank to be $1200, about at the level of traditionally much poorer Egypt. Poverty, concentrated particularly in the South and selected urban areas, is likely to continue for a considerable period of time. The direct correlation between family size and poverty suggests that any allocation programme should take the former into account. Children are a particularly vulnerable sub-set of the poor and child labour is about as high in Iraq as it is in other MENA countries such as Yemen, Morocco, and Egypt.

2) First-time job seekers and low-skilled workers: The challenge of job creation for Iraq's fast growing labour force is considerable and exacerbated by the addition of low-skilled workers who previously were employed in the public sector. Mechanisms for training and providing jobs for those most in need will be required.

3) Price regulations and subsidies: Arrangements to manage and price agricultural products in order to protect the consumer and reward Iraqi producers have to be devised. Present targeting mechanisms are inadequate, as they are in the MENA as a whole, where middle and high-income population groups have benefited disproportionately from price controls and subsidies. The poorer segments of Iraqi

rural society, including small farmers, should receive special attention.

Because poverty is particularly prevalent in rural areas; because agricultural development is vital to economic growth more generally; and because oil generated resources can greatly assist or severely impede agricultural development, a brief assessment of the agricultural sector and recommendations as to how allocations from the oil industry could best be used to benefit agriculture in the short term is included in Appendix B.

In sum, many principles of good governance and present political exigencies in Iraq support the general argument to allocate some share of national oil revenues to sub-national units of government. The devil, however, is very much in the detail of how this is accomplished. Allocations of this nature elsewhere, such as in Nigeria, Indonesia, Ecuador, Australia and Canada, reflect regional shares in the overall exploitation of the natural resource. This is particularly problematical in Iraq, however, where the presently politically excluded Sunni community also happens to be the one with least direct geographic control over oil production. Moreover, while many principles of good governance and the particularly negative experience of centralized government in Iraq support a move to decentralize, most experiences of induced decentralization have had mixed consequences for governance and democracy, to say nothing of economic development. So all that can be hoped for at this stage is that in the effort to decentralize revenue allocations, as embodied in the new constitution, for example, Iraq will not reinforce dangerous centrifugal tendencies or local non- or anti-democratic systems, and that it will not make the tasks of economic reconstruction yet more difficult. Decentralized allocations can assist in achieving positive objectives, but as the comparative record indicates, they can also have negative political and economic consequences.

Private Centralized Allocations

Although a logical possibility, allocating oil revenues through some instrumentality of the central government to private enterprises would be an almost novel approach.[1] Presumably the government would serve as a sort of investment banker, providing credit to (and possibly taking an equity position in) private enterprises. These enterprises might be in specific sectors, such as human services, infrastructure, agriculture or manufacturing. Separate governmental instrumentalities (or departments within a single one) could be established to evaluate risk and manage loans/investments in each sector. The model bears some resemblance to the consolidated German banks formed in the latter part of the 19th Century in order to mobilize and direct credit for that country's relatively late industrialization drive, or the Korean Chaebols, which were created to serve essentially the same purpose for Korea's 'late, late' development effort. Whether an Iraqi 'late, late, late' development effort could be successfully driven by a similar mechanism, in this case funded by oil revenue, is an interesting prospect to contemplate.

The model has some appealing aspects. It could utilize national resources to achieve objectives in a rational, planned fashion, much

---

1. Prior to 1979 in Iran the Shah's government did serve as an investment banker for private sector, import substitution industries, with some measure of success.

as the Germans and Koreans succeeded in doing. Sequencing of objectives will be of particular importance in Iraq's present, difficult circumstances and this model would facilitate such prioritization. The model might also achieve an appropriate balance of public and private within the economy. The state, although interventionist by virtue of its allocation of credit between alternative sectors, would leave much, if not all implementation to the private sector, possibly also fostering effective public – private relationships more generally. It could also use this mechanism to stimulate the growth of firms of varying sizes, from small to large, in different regions. As a provider of credit, the state could also insist upon transparency of accounts and procedures by private sector borrowers, presumably thereby enhancing trust and paving the way for a more effective financial system and equity markets in particular. Finally, the state could foster competition within sectors through its allocation strategies. It would also be well placed to create regulatory systems within which private sector operators would compete.

Iraqi conditions, however, may differ so greatly from those that pertained in Germany in 1900 and Korea from the late 1960s, that a model similar to that employed in those two countries might be inappropriate. One feature common to both and missing in Iraq is an effective, reasonably sized public administration. In the absence of well-trained and honest civil servants working within a public administration of appropriate size, it is difficult to imagine how a centralized instrument for credit allocation could work effectively. The Rafidain Bank, which was the state's formal mechanism for credit allocation under Saddam, certainly did not train personnel in the various skills of banking, including credit risk assessment. The Iraqi civil service as a whole was overstaffed, underpaid, and in general a far cry from the Prussian ideal. The danger that one large or several smaller credit allocation instrumentalities organized by sectors could fall prey to political or personalistic interventions is quite real. The model in any case would endow the government with very considerable leverage over the economy, leverage that it might not use wisely or well. For its part the private sector (especially that beyond a handful of 'crony capitalists') remains poorly developed in Iraq, so its capacity to put forward well developed plans upon which rational decisions by any potential lender could act, will remain limited for some time. And the very existence of a government operated credit allocation system would render it difficult, maybe to the point of impossible, for private sector banks and possibly even equity markets to compete, so the financial sector might remain underdeveloped and government-dominated.

The socio-political impacts of this approach could be negative unless at least some part of it was structured to provide capital with regard to the needs of potential beneficiaries. Heavy reliance on large scale, private sector development at an early stage of rehabilitating the Iraqi economy, especially in the absence of intensive job creation, could stimulate negative political reactions, especially among the poor. Special efforts would need to be made to ensure participation from Iraq's diverse religious/ethnic groups and that the needs of the poor were not being overlooked.

One method of diversifying beneficiaries of such a programme would be to include microfinance as a component of it. Algeria, Egypt, Morocco and Tunisia alone account for some sixty micro finance schemes, the majority of which are run by NGOs. The rationale for them is that fewer than 2 per cent of the 7.5 million poor households in the MENA (more than 60 million people) have access to formal financial services. Providing such services through NGOs would have the beneficial side effect of enhancing civil society capacities more generally.

Private Decentralized

The final alternative is no more than a logical possibility with few contemporary examples and no known present supporters, as is the case with the private, centralized model. Private, decentralized allocations of oil revenues in the form of a direct payment to citizens were mentioned by the head of the CPA as a possible alternative in his remarks to the World Economic Forum in Amman on 22 June 2003, and the relevance of the 'Alaska model,' in which a portion of pipeline revenues are paid to citizens of that state, which too was noted by Paul Bremer, has been mooted in the American media. Indeed, a poll conducted in the US after the invasion revealed that 59 per cent of likely American voters believe that this is the best way to 'rebuild the Iraqi economy and promote democracy.'[1] Numerous think tanks and Iraqi lobby groups endorsed the 'Alaska model' in the run up to the invasion and in its wake. As Iraqis have assumed more control over their country, many have endorsed the model. In sum, the broad idea of distributing at least some proportion of oil revenues directly to citizens has received more vigorous and widespread endorsement than probably any other single proposal. Before assessing its potential strengths and weaknesses in the Iraqi context, it is worth describing the 'Alaska model' in somewhat greater detail.

An 'Alaska Permanent Fund' (APF), was created by an

---

1.   www.zogby.com/news

amendment to the state constitution in 1976 after oil was discovered on the North Slope. Receiving at least one quarter of all of the state's mineral royalties, it is managed by a dedicated corporation that is overseen by a publicly appointed board of trustees and the state legislature. Its purposes are to secure future income and distribute earnings to citizens. It has had a real rate of return of over 12 per cent since the late 1980s, outpacing most other National Resource Funds.[1] Over the past several years some 600,000 Alaskan residents have received annual cheques from the APF of between one and two thousand dollars.[2]

Arguments in favour of this particular example and the 'Alaska model' more generally are presented from both good governance and broader political economy perspectives. From the former the key argument is that by enshrining the practice within the constitution, especially in such a way as to ensure oversight of the fund, particularly through an elected legislature, transparent and accountable management of oil revenues will be more likely. The proof of the pudding will be the long-term protection of the revenues and higher earnings flowing form them. The Open Society Institute, a strong supporter of this approach, cites the comparative performances of Alaska and Alberta, Canada in this regard, noting that higher rates of return in the former reflect the value added by it being enshrined in the constitution. The Alberta Heritage Savings Fund, created only through the normal legislative process, has not performed as well, because it is 'subject to the normal ups and downs of the political process.'[3]

1. Iraq Revenue Watch, 'Reports and Briefings – Protecting the Future – Constitutional Safeguards for Iraq's Oil,' (May 2005).
2. Fawaz K. Saraf, 'Oil Dividend Paper,' p. 2.
3. 'Protecting the Future,' p. 9.

From a broader political economy perspective the arguments in favour of the 'Alaska model' are more diverse and generally based on the proposition that the people, rather than their government, are to be trusted. This reasoning has strong appeal to classical liberals of the western tradition, now known in the US as conservatives or neo-conservatives, so it is not surprising that institutions such as The Heritage Foundation and the Adam Smith Institute in the UK, strongly endorse the model. But those of other political persuasions in the West and a wide variety of Iraqis do as well. The arguments of the latter tend to be of a more practical nature. So, for example, the Iraq Foundation argues that Iraqis should 'insist on the distribution of the oil money,' which should come in the form of a monthly cheque from which deductions are taken for reinvestment in the oil infrastructure, payment of the national debt and local and national taxes.[1] Not only would this manner of distributing revenues prevent 'one kleptocracy from succeeding another,' it would replace the ration system and corruption surrounding it; reduce dependence on public employment; help 'keep Iraq united and avoid the pitfalls associated with having those in power favouring one region, religious or ethnic group over others;' empower women; and undercut the insurgency.[2] Further advantages of the model, according to an American petroleum finance expert, are that it lays the foundation for a future system of progressive taxation and reduces the need for current spending in the form of income supports, subsidies or government jobs.[3] A comparatively rare dissenting view of the 'Alaska model' is that expressed in the Minority Rights Group's 'Building Democracy in

---

1. Saraf, pp. 2–3.
2. *Ibid.,* pp. 3–4.
3. Diwan, p. 28.

Iraq,' which notes that 'by translating oil revenues into hand-outs it stokes rent-seeking or competition for a larger share of those hand-outs,'[1] a point to which we shall return below.

As the insurgency has intensified and sectarian hostilities increased, the attractiveness of the 'Alaska model' has grown in some quarters, in part because of its general appeal and in part because it sidesteps the increasingly contentious issue of federalism and ensures that Sunnis will get at least their fair per capita share of oil revenues.[2] As mentioned above, the principle of private decentralized allocations may in fact have been incorporated into Article 110 of the constitution, although its wording is so vague that it is impossible to determine whether the allocations are to be to individuals or to the provincial and regional governments.

It should be noted, however, that a gathering of Iraqi political, economic and professional elites in London in the summer of 2005 expressed reservations about the 'Alaska model,' saying it was unlikely to be appropriate because Iraq does not have functioning public services so it needs public revenues to rebuild them. It also has a significant debt and massive reconstruction needs that will need all available capital for the foreseeable future.[3] It would seem in their eyes that the quarter share of revenues paid into the APF from the Alaskan oil industry exceeds that which is reasonable in the Iraqi case. Yet more robust shares as recommended by American neo-conservatives, such as the New American Foundation, which calls for 40 per cent, seem well beyond what most Iraqi elites would be willing to endorse.[4]

---

1. January 2003, p. 24.
2. This is the argument made for it by a Senior Fellow at the liberal Brookings Institution, for example. See O'Hanlon, p. 1.
3. 'Iraqi Oil Wealth,' p. 12.
4. Quoted in Saraf, p. 3.

Virtually all proposals for adoption of the 'Alaska model' ignore the profound per capita income difference between Alaska and Iraq and its consequence for the relative share of direct payments to citizens. In the former, the approximately $1,000 cheque issued in 2003 to each citizen represented about 5 per cent of each citizen's gross income. A similar check in Iraq would now represent some 80 per cent of an average citizen's income. So what in Alaska is a small top-up to individual income, possibly permitting a family holiday or appliance purchase that would not otherwise have been made, in Iraq would almost double personal income. Admittedly the Iraqi population is many times that of Alaska's, but so too will be its oil revenues once the industry is re-established. Alternatively, providing Iraqis payments based on average gross incomes similar to those in Alaska would result in annual payouts of some $50–60, hardly enough to bring profound changes in personal lives or the national political economy.

Assuming nevertheless that it is possible to erect a balanced version of the model, in which economically reasonable shares of revenues are allocated to citizens after the vital needs of government, basic social services and the oil industry are covered, there would be costs and benefits to the political economy. A practical issue would be the actual distribution mechanism, which given the extremely low level of citizen involvement in the formal banking system, even by MENA standards, would require considerable ingenuity.[1] While these allocations could be used to entice citizens into a newly

---

1. Iraq's percentage of cash outside the banking system places it on a par with other MENA 'bunker states,' i.e., Libya, Sudan, Syria and Algeria. See Clement M. Henry and Robert Springborg, *Globalization and the Politics of Development in the Middle East.* Cambridge: Cambridge University Press, 2001, p. 80.

created and presumably largely private banking system, this would be a major undertaking, implementation of which could take years. In the meantime some simpler, cruder form of allocation would have to suffice, one in which inefficiencies and possible fraud could pose major problems. Moreover, Iraq is not Alaska in the sense that it is a communally, rather than individually based society. Defining the actual beneficiary unit, whether individual, household, or otherwise, would raise many issues, not the least of which would be gender and generational rights and relations. Depending on how payments were made, they may or may not empower women.

As far as the broader economy is concerned, direct allocations could help to alleviate poverty, maybe quite substantially if payments were geared negatively to income. It is interesting to note, however, that very few of the individuals or organizations that call for the 'Alaska model' to be implemented include provisos for it to be done on a progressive basis. Possibly this is because the primary concerns of most of those endorsing it are those of good governance and political stability, rather than equity. But it is worth noting in this regard that a progressive distribution system might address long-standing Shi'a grievances against economic discrimination, which have resulted in a much higher incidence of poverty in the South than elsewhere. Indeed, the constitution calls for 'the damaged regions that were unjustly deprived' to receive higher allocations for a set period. If such allocations are to be to individuals, practical difficulties of establishing and operating such a system, which would require extensive financial information on individuals and families, might well be insurmountable. In this context it needs to be borne in mind that a system of direct personal taxation, other than at source, has never been effectively established in Iraq or, for that matter, elsewhere in the Arab world. While a distribution system may be easier to establish than a taxation one, simply because it would meet less resistance, it would still pose a very large challenge to the Iraqi state.

Putting cash directly in the hands of citizens would have mixed macroeconomic consequences. One would be to stimulate demand, which would be harmful or beneficial, depending upon the state of the economy and the capacity to meet that demand. At present, it is domestic supply, rather than demand, that is inadequate. The consequence of further demand stimulation would be an increase in import-led consumption, to say nothing of inflation. These potential liabilities might be averted were the cash payment scheme to be implemented gradually and in lock step with the recovery of the economy. Such a subtle, graduated approach would be both a challenge to implement, however, and be beyond the understanding of most Iraqis, hence unpopular at least among those clamouring for immediate 'entitlements.' Direct payments could of course be used to stimulate demand as part of that recovery process, were inadequate demand to be seen as an obstacle to more rapid recovery, which does not seem the case at present. Moreover, once a level of payment was established, it would become an entitlement that would be difficult or impossible to utilize as a tool of flexible, macroeconomic management. In sum, at this stage of reconstruction implementation of the 'Alaska model' might well stimulate further demand for imported commodities and feed inflation, consequences that would probably more than offset whatever benefits would be derived from further demand stimulation. A progressive Alaska type system would possibly not have quite such negative macroeconomic consequences, for the poor presumably would be less likely to purchase imported goods, depending primarily on the ability of the Iraqi agricultural sector to satisfy demand.

The impact on savings and investment of this allocation scheme would probably be negative, especially if it were operated on a progressive basis. In that case consumption would be particularly enhanced, with a concomitant reduction in national savings and investment, although demand creation could go some way to stimulate investment, presumably especially of a private nature in the foodstuffs, construction, clothing, and other personal consumption industries.[1] It would be investment in national, probably governmental projects, such as those in human and physical infrastructure, that would could be most negatively affected, depending on the proportion of total revenues retained directly by the state or gained by it through taxation of private operators.

Finally, it could be argued that entitlements, especially when provided without regard to need, militate against the development of personal economic independence, entrepreneurialism and attitudes supportive of both. Presumably any correlation between entitlements and these alleged negative side effects would depend in considerable measure on the size of those entitlements relative to the total personal income of recipients.

The chief political advantage of allocating some portion of oil

---

1. Stimulating agricultural production should be a very high priority and if this type of allocation system contributed to that objective, it would be a marked advantage. Not only would an expanding agricultural sector make a signal contribution to reducing unemployment, it would also feed into the foodstuffs industry, which was an exporting sector into the early 1980s.

revenues directly to citizens is apparently seen by its proponents as gaining support for the incumbent political system. It would do so because it would be seen as having provided an immediate material benefit and because this measure would signal the rulers' recognition that the national oil patrimony belonged to the people of Iraq. This reasoning seems sound, although gratuitous payments tend to be perceived over time as entitlements, thereby reducing their immediate, tangible political benefit for governments, while making it politically risky for them to reduce or remove those entitlements. But in conditions of extreme need, as seems now to be the case in Iraq, urgent requirements of political popularity and legitimacy may be such that the long-term consequences of entitlements are simply costs that have to be borne. It goes without saying that any government that would seek to commit any significant share of the country's oil earnings to the 'Alaska model' would have to be viewed as legitimate and fully empowered to do so, something which the present government is not. A premature attempt to bolster governmental legitimacy through such allocations could possibly backfire.

A final possible political advantage of this method of allocation is that it might indeed tip the balance of power in the direction of civil society, away from the state. Because allocations would take the form of entitlements, they would preclude administrative or political discretion, hence their conversion into patronage, the lifeblood of authoritarianism. The availability of regular, guaranteed payments might also prove to be a resource into which civil society organizations could tap, making appeals for individuals to contribute some portion of those payments. Even without organized activities of this sort, the relative shift of expenditure of resources from the discretionary power of the state to that of individuals might provide resources for civil society. Providing Iraqis an economic right to payment from oil revenues might reinforce a sense of political rights, or at least establish a precedent of separating support from the state from an obligation of fealty to incumbent elites.

Conclusion

Each of these possible approaches has costs and benefits. To improve the ratio of the former over the latter, combinations of the approaches could be used. So, for example, some portion of oil revenues could be used to support Alaskan style payments to citizens, while another portion could be reserved for use by an autonomous, governmental development body or for allocation by a government investment fund. Indeed, many thoughtful analyses of the 'Alaska model' suggest it be used in such combinations. Roger Diwan, for example, suggests a tripartite division of revenues, with profits from the INOC being controlled directly by parliament and used for governmental purposes; tax earnings from Production Sharing Agreements being dedicated initially to reconstruction and social funds, subsequently to a fund for future generations; and royalty payments dispersed directly to the population, a la Alaska.[1] The Iraq Foundation proposes a yet more elaborate system, in which each citizen would receive a monthly account and cheque, in which information about deductions from his/her gross payment for reinvestment in the oil infrastructure, debt payments, local and national taxes, and any other charges, would be itemized.[2]

---

1. Diwan.
2. Saraf.

But whether thoroughbred or hybrid, the most critical criterion for the evaluation of any option from a political economy perspective is its ability to contribute to the construction and maintenance of the state's legal and administrative frameworks, without which free markets and democratic politics cannot function. These frameworks include reasonably depoliticised and effective public administrations at national and sub-national levels; taxation systems capable of extracting resources from payees in a legal, fair and efficient fashion; regulatory systems that enforce requirements of transparency and accountability on economic actors; and representative policy making institutions that operate in free and fair fashion to convert competitive policy preferences into enforceable laws and regulations. In the absence of these state capacities, which cannot be sustained without free and fair elections, neither private enterprise nor civil society can flourish.

In Iraq, where the state has never succeeded in constructing and maintaining these enabling legal and administrative frameworks, and where it degenerated under Saddam into a brutal mechanism for totalitarian control by a privileged clan, it may be tempting to devalue the important and positive contributions the state must make if Iraq is ultimately to enjoy democracy and a prosperous, free market economy. Because individual Iraqis and civil society were crushed under the Ba'th, it may seem both just and effective to utilize oil resources to benefit them directly and, in relation to the state, disproportionately. This would be a mistake. Civil society cannot flourish under an authoritarian state, or one too weak to establish and enforce reasonable rules for political competition. A viable market economy will not emerge in the absence of effective legal and administrative structures, regardless of how much money consumers have in their pockets. To wreak vengeance, intentional or otherwise, on the Iraqi state because of the previous excesses of its rulers, would be to perpetuate the sufferings of its people. Its reconstruction is a precondition for their collective economic and political success. And its reconstruction will depend in very large measure on the effective utilization of oil revenues.

In sum, radical application of the 'Alaskan model' would probably undermine reconstruction efforts, both political and economic. More limited applications, tied closely to efforts to create effective governance while stimulating economic recovery, are more appropriate and seem to be more likely to engender adequate political support in Iraq. What is required is more thorough analysis of various options from both economic and political perspectives. The sort of careful political economy research that is necessary for effective policy making is clearly beyond the capacities of Iraq at the present time. This in turn increases the danger of poor policies being made as a result of lack of adequate information and analysis, on the one hand, and heightened political tension and demands, on the other. No area is most susceptible to these problems than is that of allocation of oil revenues.

Ownership

The international oil market, especially low cost Middle East oil, has always been regulated – prior to the formation of OPEC by the international oil cartel, and since the 1960s by a combination of oil producing and oil consuming associations. OPEC has played a particularly important role in regulating the output of the low-cost, high reserve and capacity Middle Eastern producers. Such regulation of Middle East oil production is of utmost importance, precisely because of the low cost and high reserves in the region. Without such regulation, although oil prices might fall in the short term, over the longer term they could become yet more unstable, disadvantaging both producers and consumers.

It is vital, therefore, that at this critical juncture in Iraq's history, decisions regarding investment, output and pricing of oil need to be made within a national strategy which ensures optimal extraction and prices of oil in the long run. Fragmentation of the industry, which would impair coherence in strategic decision-making, should be avoided. The primary role of the Ministry of Oil in the design of a unified national strategy, and the secondary role of the INOC as implementer, will remain critical unless and until new institutions to manage oil policy are created. Whatever form they take, unified, authoritative, and well informed national oil institutions are necessary to protect the interests of Iraq in dealings with foreign oil companies and by so doing, reinforce the legitimacy of the Iraqi government.

This is not to suggest that reform of the Iraqi oil industry is unnecessary. Indeed, such reform is vital if Iraqi interests are to be adequately served. Like some other national oil companies in the Middle East, the INOC has failed to expand Iraqi production effectively, while the government, acting primarily through the Ministry of Oil, distorted and rendered inefficient the local energy market. Many other countries in the region are now trying to deal with these same problems by outsourcing various commercial activities of their national oil companies to private service contractors, or by entering into production sharing agreements with IOCs, and by reducing energy subsidies. The current situation is a golden opportunity for Iraq to liberalize its domestic energy market and to reconceptualize the role of the INOC.[1]

---

1.   Reduction or removal of subsidies on energy, food, and other commodities and services should be related to the growth of the economy and reduction of need. At present, estimates place unemployment at some two thirds of the labour force. Poverty is particularly severe in rural Iraq, where, according to a January 2003 World Bank report, more than one half of the population does not have access to safe water (compared to 85 per cent who enjoy such access in urban areas). Targeting subsidies on the poor, especially its rural component, is probably not an option in the short or even medium term, so the economic costs and inefficiencies of subsidizing the entire population will have to be borne for some time. But the oil industry could set an example by making such subsidies transparent and separate from the production function. So in the case, for example, of oil refineries oriented primarily to export markets and managed on economic rather than political criteria, they could sell fixed

In sum, the development of the Iraqi oil industry should be within the framework of a coherent national strategy in order to prevent undue instability in international oil markets and to safeguard the long-term national interests of Iraq. The country should remain within OPEC, where an appropriate bargain might be struck between the future market share for Iraq and the reduction or writing off of Iraq's outstanding debt to Arab oil exporting countries. But within these parameters, there is very considerable scope for the overhaul of the Iraqi oil industry to make it more efficient, while also rendering it more supportive of the development of democracy. Finally, it should be emphasized that the key to Iraqi economic development is to establish linkages between the oil industry and the remainder of the economy in ways that will stimulate the growth of the private sector.[1] If the reconstruction of the Iraqi oil industry reproduces its previous enclave status, it will have failed no matter how efficient that industry becomes.

The present legal/administrative structure of the oil industry was established over the thirty-five years of Saddam's rule. The Iraqi industry as a whole was controlled by the Ministry of Oil through the INOC. It consisted of two major production companies, North and South Oil, which had responsibilities for fields in their

---

quantities of product to domestic distributors at subsidized prices.

1.   It will probably be necessary for Iraq to adopt specifically designed policies to achieve that end, for the enclave nature of the industry tends naturally to militate against such linkages. Possibly the best example of a crafted policy intended to utilize the dynamic of the oil industry to drive the development of others is that of Norway, where by law oil companies must procure 70 per cent of their goods and services from Norwegian sources. As a result, over 4,000 private Norwegian companies supply the oil sector, including significant numbers of manufacturing companies. See 'Iraqi Oil Wealth,' p. 11.

geographic areas; a company for oil projects, which was for design and engineering of upstream and downstream activities; an oil exploration company; a marketing company; a tanker company; and various departments in the ministry, which ran the pipeline system, distributed oil products, and operated downstream LPG projects. In 2001 a company was created to oversee development of new fields.

The following four-celled table identifies possible alternatives for the ownership structure of the Iraqi oil industry.

Ownership

	Public	Private
Centralized	INOC	INOC privatized to anchor investor(s) or PSAs
Decentralized	Ownership by province/region or Sector ('unbundling')	Privatized by subsector or region

Public Centralized

This alternative is a yet more restrictive version of the status quo, for in fact Iraq has already entered into production sharing agreements (PSAs) with Russian, Chinese and other, including French oil companies, which for all intents and purposes transfer ownership of Iraqi oil to them. The legal status of these agreements, however, signed as they were during the sanctions regime and possibly out of the political motivation of influencing the permanent members of the UN Security Council, remains in doubt. Prior to the war, Iraq itself apparently abrogated most, if not all of these agreements on the basis that the companies concerned had not fulfilled contractual obligations to commence explorations and/or exploitation. It is possible, however, that a substantial body of Iraqi opinion, possibly driven by nationalism and in some cases, self interest, will support a restoration of the status quo ante, whereby the Ministry of Oil, possibly by virtue of a constitutional provision, would preside over state owned companies responsible for all aspects of the oil industry from production to marketing. Those companies would enter into service contracts with private, including foreign firms, but would not assign shares of oil production to them.

It was this model, used throughout most of the Ba'thist era, that enabled that elite to convert oil revenues into the political patronage that played such a vital role in perpetuating its rule, while also impeding the effective and rapid development of the oil industry. If it were resuscitated it could once again contribute to the concentration of political power, while having uncertain impacts on the oil industry itself. It might also have a negative effect on the economy more generally because it would recreate conditions in which the Dutch disease flourishes. Paradoxically, however, in the short term this model might facilitate access to international capital. Any borrowing to upgrade the industry will require a level of legal certainty as to the legitimacy of the underlying obligations and rights being funded or supported by the lending. Lending institutions will require no less, as will agencies that issue political risk insurance. So lending to support projects that are legally questionable, such as purchasing oil assets through some type of privatization, is unlikely to occur soon. So a reconstituted INOC may actually be more able to engage in borrowing because its legal title and rights are better established, although it, too, would be subject to present international restrictions.

In this 'status quo' model, access to technology could be obtained through service contracts with foreign oil companies, which could be repaid from the proceeds of oil sales. It is possible to obtain modern technology in this way, but careful crafting and management of those contracts is essential. If technical specifications and requirements are well set out and the company chosen, for example, to build a new facility, is required to grant the INOC the relevant licenses to use the technology in question, then technical modernization of the INOC could ensue. If it had procurement rules providing for competitive and effective bidding and a sound final contract, the invitations to bid could also create effective price competition. Present high oil prices do not guarantee, but they render it much more likely that Iraq would be able to borrow sufficient monies against future oil production in order to rebuild and expand its oil industry in this manner.

This best-case scenario of the public ownership model, however, may well be difficult to implement. One potential problem is that companies paid fees for services, rather than sharing in development risks and potential rewards, are less committed. The so-called 'buy-back' model, a version of this approach, has amply demonstrated its weaknesses in neighbouring Iran. It encourages neither utilization of up to date technology nor cost cutting, for costs and fees are fixed. If Iraq were to choose this option, it might protract the country's reconstruction.

But even if it avoids the pitfalls of the buyback system, the challenge of operating a large oil industry on the basis of numerous service contracts with a plethora of foreign companies is prodigious.

This is precisely why many countries, including Russia, for example, permit large IOCs to buy into their oil industries. They seek from them not only infusions of technology, as well as capital and human resource development, but they also hope to obtain assistance for their overall management of the industry. In Iraq's present situation of resource shortages of all sorts and in the wake of an extended period of quasi-isolation from the international energy system, its capacity to provide optimal management of the oil sector, including forward planning, is very doubtful. A possible outcome of borrowing against future earnings and subcontracting specific tasks is that of suboptimal overall management and development of the industry, thus rendering this approach cost ineffective in the long term.

An associated economic problem is that despite the ability to borrow against future oil earnings there may well be a scarcity of resources for the oil industry, simply because of intense competition with other needs, such as direct distribution to an impoverished, politically active population. As long as the government is in direct control of the industry, without a substantial barrier between it and commercial operations, the temptation to draw upon the oil resource to finance needs not related to that industry, are substantial. This is precisely what the Ba'thist regime in fact did. Competitive needs for governmental revenues during the last dozen years of Saddam's regime contributed substantially to the present dilapidated state of the oil infrastructure. A similar approach now could seriously hamper reconstruction of the oil industry. Indeed, there is substantial evidence to suggest that is what is occurring, as funds nominally earmarked for maintenance and operations appear to be siphoned off into other expenditures.[1]

---

1.   See note 1, p. 14.

The political downsides of the variations of the publicly centralized model of ownership are potentially more significant than the economic ones. Although it is unlikely that direct state control and operation of the oil industry would reproduce as bad a political outcome as it contributed to under Ba'thism, it is also improbable that it would make a positive contribution to the emergence of political pluralism. As long as virtually all oil revenues are flowing directly to the state, the tendency for them to be converted into political patronage to sustain incumbent elites is profound. While various constitutional, legal and institutional devices might be put in place to guard against this development, that sort of infrastructure would be novel and untested in Iraq. By itself it likely would be inadequate to prevent both the misuse of oil revenues and their utilization for political purposes. Additional bulwarks of an economic and political nature would be necessary, including a reasonable effective system of direct taxation, a competent public administration, and budgetary/accounting systems controlled by an elected body with the political strength to stand up to the executive. In circumstances of protracted scarcity, compounded by economic and political centralization, reinforced by complete control over oil resources, such economic/political/administrative development would be very difficult to achieve, especially if there are no existing foundations for such. Iraq, without any of these requisites for the constraint of authoritarian government based on oil rents, is unlikely to develop them in the face of the resurrection of an oil economy that helped prevent their emergence in the past.

In sum, Iraq could seek to preserve total state ownership of its oil industry and to modernize it through service contracts, in which case it would face a challenge to gain access to state of the art technology and might also encounter difficulties in accessing capital. It would also face obstacles in the development of capacity to provide up to date, day-to-day management of the industry. Most importantly and least apparent, because of its lack of capacity and experience, it might forego the opportunity to plan and then implement the long term, integrated development of the energy industry, hence fail to extract maximum benefits for Iraq from its enormously valuable hydrocarbon resources.

Alternatively, Iraq might cede more control over its oil resources by entering into some form of licensing agreements equivalent to Iran's buy-back system. Unless and until governmental stability and legitimacy are firmly established, however, such agreements are unlikely to be signed with any but the least risk-averse international oil companies, those with the lowest level of professionalism. This approach in Iran, moreover, has not resulted in IOCs making really substantial improvements to that country's oil production and processing. In the case of a continuation of centralized, state ownership of the oil industry, there is considerable danger that revenues will again be converted into political patronage, thereby militating against democratization. Moreover, the centralized, state controlled oil-industry that failed under Saddam to serve as an engine of growth for the broader economy, would probably fail to do so again.

Public Decentralized

A main feature of MENA oil economies is their extreme centralization, manifested in one or two large urban centres, which are also the seat of political power, growing in a hothouse manner by virtue of being the main beneficiaries of the expenditure of oil rents. The attraction of the working age population to these urban centres handicaps social and economic development of outlying regions, and militates against the full utilization and development of other resources in the economy. Consequently, the economy becomes increasingly dependent on oil revenues and the state increasingly perceived as the creator and guarantor of jobs. Oil becomes the lifeblood of the economy, the state its heart. As a result, with the collapse of the state, as in present day Iraq, economic life is paralysed. One of the principal aims of Iraqi reconstruction should be to prevent the reconstitution of a highly centralized, oil dependent economy that devalues other resources and outlying regions, and to accomplish this without fragmenting the body politic along geographic lines or impeding the formation of a coherent national oil policy.

Decentralizing the oil industry could make signal contributions to decentralizing the economy and stimulating its regional components. Historically the Ministry of Oil's two major state oil production companies, North and South Oil, focus on northern and southern oil fields, which contain 20 and 80 per cent of Iraq's current production, respectively. While their field operations have been in those regions, their management and control have been centralized in Baghdad. Devolving their management to the provinces in which they operate and doing the same with the comparatively recently established state company responsible for developing new oil fields, might succeed in distributing oil industry personnel, including management, to areas outside Baghdad and do so in a more balanced geographic fashion than if just the North and South Oil companies were to undergo some form of managerial devolution. Deconcentration of management and operations, coupled with continuing state ownership, might produce some of the economic benefits of decentralization while posing less of a risk to political fragmentation than would be the case were actual ownership to be handed over to provinces or regions.

But such devolution/decentralization would require extensive reorganization and local capacity building. It would beg various questions about the structure of relationships between Baghdad and regional operations, one example of which would be the choice of where to situate regional headquarters, with the choice of Mosul versus Kirkuk in the North being but one example of the profound political implications of such choices. It would not be easy to establish effective, coordinated, decentralized operations and their very existence might threaten the coherence of national oil policy. It is, nevertheless, at least hypothetically possible.[1]

It might be easier simply to 'unbundle' some of the services associated with upstream production, not to mention downstream petroleum and gas distribution systems. This could be a first step toward privatization, discussed below. The political consequences of unbundling various services, even while retaining the state's ownership of them, could be reasonably positive. The more the oil labour force and its operations are geographically dispersed, the more their presence and the resources that presence brings

---

1. PEMEX, the Mexican state-owned oil company, is one of the few to have been subject to decentralization, a process that commenced in the 1990s after several years of study. It involved relocating the principal offices and workforces of two of the four operating companies (petrochemicals, exploration and production) to outlying regions close to actual production sites. It was made possible by a previous 'unbundling' of PEMEX's operations.

can contribute to invigorating provincial and local economies and government. Coupled with some form of revenue sharing with provinces, this model has the possibility of tilting the balance of power away from Baghdad toward the periphery, while not necessarily threatening fragmentation of the national polity. The actual and symbolic importance of the central state retaining ownership might be particularly important in this regard, especially for the immediate and even mid-term futures. To decentralize ownership of the existing state companies would entail much greater risk in this regard, especially in light of Sunni apprehensions having been heightened by the wording of relevant articles in the new constitution.

In sum, decentralizing ownership of oil resources to sub-national geographic units, whether provinces or otherwise, risks political fragmentation and the coherence of national oil policy. It would be strongly opposed by
s and many other Iraqis. But the alternative of unbundling some oil services would be less controversial, and it might achieve comparable economic and political benefits for outlying regions. Comparative investigations of other national oil industries would reveal how much decentralization might be achieved in what traditionally has been a highly centralized industry, as opposed to what has been accomplished in several countries through unbundling. Appendix C, 'Unbundling Oil Services in Algeria,' summarizes the comparative experience of this North African state, which has achieved some success in unbundling its oil industry over the past fifteen years or so, although progress has not been unilinear, nor has it yet successfully paved the way for privatization, a logical follow on step.

Private Centralized

At least two possible models exist within this category. One is the privatization en bloc of some percentage or all of the key holding company, the INOC, possibly also including in that privatization some of the operational departments presently within the Ministry of Oil. In 2001, for example, Norway privatized 18.5 per cent of the state-owned mega-company Statoil, more of which may be privatized in the future. Theoretically Iraq could follow this example, privatizing a portion of the INOC now, possibly to one or more anchor investors, in order to gain quick access to capital and technology for the oil industry, as well as substantial resources for more general development and budgetary support. An effort could be made to draw in a mixed group of such anchor investors, as well as Iraqis, thereby averting possible criticism that the nation's oil patrimony was being surrendered to foreigners. Further privatizations could subsequently be undertaken if the initial one was deemed to be a success. The state could of course retain majority ownership.

Iraq, however, is not Norway. No equivalent developing country has recently privatized its oil industry in this fashion, presumably because of nationalist considerations. If Iraq were to do so its political leadership would probably come under intense criticism from within Iraq, the Middle East, and even beyond. Moreover, such an ambitious and novel departure would require profound trust on the part of investors as well as the Iraqis themselves, trust that would have to be based on perceptions of an effective governmental, including legal-judicial system. Assuming such a system will emerge over the next few years, it would still take some years thereafter to negotiate a privatization of this profile.

A centralized privatization is not a quick or politically easy fix to what ails the Iraqi oil industry.

Assuming the political storm privatization would stimulate could be withstood, the longer term political consequences would be mixed. On the one hand, the need to create effective legal-judicial, taxation and regulatory systems to make a large scale oil privatization possible would presumably have spill over effects into the political economy more generally. In this scenario, privatization would be a driver of general administrative and governmental reform. Presumably this would require a core 'change team' of technocrats, backed by a firmly established political elite, to design and implement the needed reforms. Again, it seems unlikely that either a key team of technocrats or a coherent, firmly established and representative political elite is likely to be established in the foreseeable future, so again this option is not one on the immediate horizon.

Negative political consequences might also flow from privatization. The state would continue to directly obtain an overwhelming share of oil revenues, so unless that state were subject to the rule of law, those revenues would likely become patronage resources. A privatization of this nature would do nothing to counteract the present condition of over-centralization of the oil-based economy. Privatization involving foreign investors would probably stimulate anti-Iraqi sentiments and actions among other MENA producers, thereby creating foreign policy problems and possibly accentuating internal schisms as external actors might seek to 'stir up trouble' in Iraq.

In sum, a bold, centralized privatization would be a profound, risky step, which to succeed would require time, a capable team of technocrats and a political elite with enough of a base and sufficient courage to support the politically challenging undertaking. It would also require the development of effective systems of governance if the private components of the oil industry were to be effectively taxed and regulated. This is a demanding requirement for a country in Iraq's present shape, so is probably one that should be thought of as being appropriate only at a later stage, if at all. If the structures of governance necessary for effective privatization began to emerge, then this could be read as a sign that this option might be considered.

A less innovative, provocative means of privatization would be for the INOC to enter into production sharing agreements (PSAs) with foreign concerns.[1] While they can award a share of oil production resulting from exploration/development activities to the private partner, they can also provide other forms of compensation that are not so obviously a transfer of ownership of the oil produced. One such method is a discount on the price of crude purchased by the private partner from the national oil company owner.

MENA producers, especially the large Gulf ones, have been reluctant to enter into PSAs, in part because nationalists see them as a return to the bad old days of oil concessions, in which foreigners for all intents and purposes owned MENA oil, and in part because of the personal interests of those presently working for or otherwise benefiting directly from state owned oil companies in those countries. It is the case, however, that some MENA producers, including Algeria, Egypt and Libya, entered into PSAs some years ago and that some of the large Gulf producers have

---

1. Production Sharing Agreements (PSAs) are also known as Production Sharing Contracts (PSCs).

recently done so as well.[1] Interestingly, Iraq began entering into PSAs in 1997, when it signed agreements with the China National Petroleum Company for the al-Ahdab field and with Lukoil, which headed a group of Russian companies, for the West Qurna field. By October 2002, Deutsche Bank estimated that the Iraqi government had concluded deals with as many as thirty foreign oil companies, of which many were based on production sharing agreement principles.[2] Being under the duress of sanctions at the time, Iraq had particular motives for entering into PSAs, and has already unilaterally abrogated several of those contracts. Whether present informed Iraqi sentiment is to reject PSAs in principle, or just particular ones, is unknown.

A strategy to develop Iraqi oil resources based on PSAs implies

---

1. Algeria has toyed with PSAs since 1986. A law passed in that year after intense deliberations permitted PSAs as long as Sonatrach held the majority of the shares in equity oil. Amendments in 1991 sweetened the taxation and royalty provisions and for the first time offered key incentives to attract investment in the upstream gas sector, hitherto closed to foreign companies. Substantial foreign investment resulted, along with the discovery of new fields that made Algeria, along with Norway, the second most prolific region in the world (measured by the ratio of new crude oil reserves to exploratory wells) after Angola in 1994–8. But by 2000 Algeria was producing more oil than new reserves to cover it. IOCs most capable of ambitious investments want higher returns than Algeria's present system can provide. IOCs also object to the difficulties of dealing with Sonatrach. In its present form the national oil company plays a variety of incompatible roles. It is state arbiter, joint venture partner, and sometimes also holds an independent stake in the enterprise shared with the joint venture. Algeria's hybrid oil industry cannot attract the multi-billion dollar investments that BP, for instance, staked in its 2003 joint venture in Russia. As an example of the recent spread of PSAs into the Gulf, Kuwait signed a major PSA with Shell in 2003. See Carola Hoyos, 'Gulf Oil Countries Hint at a New World of Opportunity,' *Financial Times* (23 July 2003), 18.

2. Roberts, p. 11.

lower thresholds for supportive legal-judicial and governance structures more generally than does the full-blown privatization model just discussed, as evidenced by the fact that several such agreements were signed under Saddam's regime, although at what discount rate is unknown. Nevertheless, major international oil companies will require some assurances in the form of a legitimate government with some manifestations of a rule of law, so like the privatization model, the PSA one would provide a stimulus for such development more broadly.[1] On the other hand, just like in the case of full-blown privatization, PSAs do not result in a distribution of resources geographically or from the state to private interests, including civil society. It is perfectly possible then, that a PSA based strategy could result in a minimally effective system of centralized governance being the recipient of 100 per cent of the oil revenues accruing to Iraq. The PSA model does not even necessitate elaboration of the virtually non-existent taxation system, as a privatization model does at least in a limited way.

The PSA approach, although politically more acceptable in Iraq and the MENA than privatization, would face at least some domestic and regional political criticism.[2] Such criticism, however, might in the long run not be as important as the fact that it would not by itself bring about any fundamental changes in the

---

1. Whether in the form of PSAs or other types of privatization, the level of transparency that eventuates between international oil companies and the government of Iraq will be paramount in the management of oil revenues and for the improvement of governance. The Extractive Industries Transparency Initiative (EITI), which seeks agreed standards, covering oil, gas and mining, could be of particular importance in the Iraqi context, were it to come to fruition.

2. See for example 'Iraqis Losing out on Oil Fortune,' which cites a report that PSAs could lead to a $113 billion 'rip-off' of Iraq by INOCs. http://english.aljazeera.net/english/DialogueBox (22 November 2005).

structure of domestic ownership or allocation of resources of the oil industry, unless it were coupled with other specific changes to those allocations.[1] The PSA approach tends to divorce overhaul of the oil industry from reform of the polity, thereby depriving the latter of a driving force for change. While it may be the most economically sound approach, in that it mobilizes exogenous capital and technology and maintains ultimate Iraqi control over its oil resources (PSAs are typically for fixed time periods) while preserving centralized decision making over oil policy as a whole, it does not reinforce political reform and could in fact work against it.

Private Decentralized

This is the neo-liberal model most commonly advocated by those of that persuasion in the West, especially the US. The Heritage Foundation, for example, advocates 'the Oil Ministry and regional oil companies should be restructured to transform them into attractive government-owned oil companies as an intermediary stage before initial public offering (IPO).' It goes on to spell the proposal out in somewhat greater detail, suggesting that there be three geographically based companies (south, central, north) and three additional companies, one each for pipelines, refineries, and

---

1. It is theoretically possible, for example, to earmark revenues from PSAs for social or other purposes. Similarly, PSAs could involve 'offsets' that would require foreign partners to engage in other economic sectors, possibly in a way with direct social benefits. In Algeria, for example, BP is compelled by virtue of its contract with the state oil company Sonatrach to export artisanal products on behalf of a local handicrafts programme. Sonatrach itself is drawing upon revenues obtained from oil sales to improve social facilities in villages in oil producing areas.

natural gas.[1] These divisions correspond roughly, but not exactly, to existing companies and departments, hence the 'restructuring' referred to above.

The Iraq Foundation, composed primarily of Iraqi exiles in the US, endorses the model of decentralized privatization, arguing that 'it is only by shifting these assets (the 80 per cent of total productive assets controlled by the state) squarely back into the private sector that the economy will be properly invigorated.'[2] It however cautions that privatization is 'fraught with pitfalls' and recommends a variety of steps to ensure that it is done properly. These steps include partial and deferred valuation (so that assets not be sold cheaply under duress); vouchers (which it recognizes went awry in Eastern Europe but believes such a system could be used effectively to 're-distribute wealth at a grass roots level'); de-nationalization (return of confiscated/nationalized business assets to their original owners on the condition that they modernize and upgrade them); and offset programmes (to compel foreign investors in the oil industry to invest in non-oil sectors of the economy). In each case the Iraq Foundation recognizes that these programmes have been found wanting in previous applications, but argues that with remedial measures they could be made to work effectively in Iraq. Clearly implied is that privatization will be to both Iraqi and foreign investors.

The more decentralized (i.e., segmented) the privatization, the less political obstacles it would confront and the more potentially

---

1. Ariel Cohen and Gerald P. O'Driscoll, 'The Road to Economic Prosperity for a Post-Saddam Iraq,' www.heritage.org/Research/MiddleEast/bgl633.cfm

2. Basim al-Rahim, 'Notes on Iraq,' www.iraqfoundation.org/studies/2003/afeb/10_reconstruction.html

beneficial economic and political repercussions it might have. The Heritage Foundation proposal creates three regionally based, major production companies. This could exacerbate intra-ethnic and intra-religious tensions and would in any case result in very large companies indeed as measured by their total reserves, hence likely to stimulate considerable political opposition. From both political and economic perspectives it would seem advisable to slice the pie into more pieces, both geographically and functionally. There is no particular reason, other than the political one of winning support for change, to allow monopolies in these functions. Indeed, it might well be argued that structured competition would be more favourable from both economic and political perspectives. Moreover, there is no compelling need to privatize entire sub-components, whether geographic or functional. The continued existence of publicly owned companies would serve both political ends and provide competition for private operators, hence a means to control and evaluate their performance. The need to create effective regulatory frameworks would certainly be enhanced by the very complexity of a mixed, public-private industry.

A gradual, segmented privatization programme would presumably bring about less of a political backlash. Precisely because it would be 'componentized' it could commence earlier than one that was conceived of in larger slices. Its management would be complex, but that could be a further stimulus for erecting regulatory structures and mechanisms, which would hopefully also contribute to the development of the rule of law more broadly.

This approach might also be more compatible with strategies to shift control over oil revenues from the centralized state to non-national governmental levels and to private Iraqi citizens. With more privatizations it would be easier to create a greater mix of beneficiaries/participants, while reducing the chances that a limited number of actors could seize great advantage from the process, a la Russia. Earmarks in the form of ownership or payments from sale proceeds could be provided to non-national units of government in order to facilitate revenue sharing, and they could also be provided in some form to individual Iraqis. A complex and diverse approach would provide opportunities to benefit numerous constituencies, while also providing some economic basis for political pluralism.

'Unbundling' monolithic, state-owned oil sectors, either as a means to decentralize public ownership or as a preparatory step for partial or complete privatization, is a challenge Algeria, Mexico, and numerous other countries currently are confronting. In the latter, Article 27, paragraph 4 of the 1917 constitution stipulates, 'the nation shall have direct title and ownership of petroleum and all solid, liquid and gaseous hydrocarbons.' This provision is further reinforced by accompanying regulatory laws. The way in which Mexican decision makers are seeking to square the circle between this provision and their desire to privatize some portion of PEMEX, the state owned oil monolith, is to do so a long way downstream, as far from the upstream, production end as possible, e.g., in 'secondary' petrochemicals and the transportation and distribution of gas.[1] Not as closely restricted by law as Mexico, Algeria has for many years been toying with privatization of components of Sonatrach that are somewhat closer to the

---

1.   As far as actual sales of assets are concerned, PEMEX has only sold 51 per cent of its lubricants subsidiary and all of its air fleet. Other 'privatizations' have taken the form of opening up of some downstream operations to private concerns, such as petrochemicals, transportation and distribution of fuels and natural gas, ownership of service stations, and LNG facilities.

upstream end. It has in fact 'spun off' several companies, including ENAGEO, which conducts geophysical surveys. It remains a public sector company, but like other such spin-offs, it apparently will be privatized when and if pending legislation is passed.

These and other cases of spinning off and then privatizing downstream and, in some instances, upstream components of state owned oil industries, suggest a possible model for Iraq. Mexico and Algeria have sought to ensure that their nationals are in a position to play key roles in newly privatized companies. Iraq, with skilled manpower in the oil sector, is in a position to do likewise. It could 'unbundle' both upstream activities, such as geophysical analyses, drilling, well service and maintenance, and, moving downstream, pipeline construction, refining, transport, and so on. Iraqi engineers and technicians could then be provided loans from the INOC or a state fund as described above to purchase or start up such companies, possibly in joint ventures with outsiders. In this fashion the oil sector would have a positive impact on the nascent private sector and would link the petroleum enclave to the rest of the economy. The final step of privatization, following the 'unbundling,' would also facilitate technology transfer through joint ventures in which Iraqi experts would play a vital role.

The major potential downside of this decentralized approach to privatization is that its very complexity would make it hard to organize, manage and implement, possibly resulting in problems that would bring the whole process into disrepute and result in undesired, unintended consequences. Even though this type of privatization would lend itself to a gradual, piecemeal approach, it might just be too much for a newly emerging Iraqi government to handle, even with substantial foreign technical assistance.

And if problems arose, the very involvement of that foreign assistance might give rise to charges of 'guilt by association,' thus undermining governmental legitimacy.

It is also possible that by fragmenting the oil industry and privatizing some if not all of its components, overall policy control of the industry would be substantially diminished or altogether lost. While such has not occurred in Algeria or Mexico, they have just started down this path and in the latter, where privatization has taken place, it remains concentrated downstream. Algeria's 'unbundling' has yet to be followed with systematic privatizations, other than of petrol stations. Iraq's immediate needs are more upstream, so if privatization is going to have a big and beneficial impact on the Iraqi oil industry, it will need to embrace more upstream activity than has been the case in Mexico. As a simple rule of thumb it would seem wise for a decentralized privatization of this sort to proceed in measured, incremental fashion, so that capacity to manage a more complex, diverse, not entirely state owned industry could develop in tandem with the privatization. No other MENA producer has undertaken a thorough privatization in this fashion, so there is no regional reference point which could serve as an overall guide, although limited unbundlings and privatizations have taken place in the MENA and they could inform Iraqi deliberations.

Conclusion

The preceding discussion has identified alternative models of ownership and evaluated them from a political economy perspective in somewhat impressionistic, non-structured fashion. The evaluative criteria referred to include the impact of the model on the balance, both political and economic, between the state and non-state actors (including civil society) and between the governmental centre and periphery. Other criteria are whether the model would contribute to politically centrifugal or centripetal forces; would support or undermine legal/regulatory institutions and processes; and would facilitate or undermine the coherence of national policy making for the hydrocarbon sector. Economic criteria referred to include whether or not the ownership model would provide access to capital and technology; would contribute to an effective balance between public and private sectors; would stimulate growth of the private sector; and could be implemented within a reasonable time frame. Lastly, the potential social impacts of alternative models have been referred to, although in the absence of reliable, up to date social data it is difficult to be very precise in this regard.

Without attempting to be more rigorous, such as by creating a scale and quantifying the scores of the various models along the political, economic and social dimensions, it is possible to observe that the public centralized model, which is more or less to retain the present structure, has significant political and economic disadvantages; and that the private centralized one in the form of an en bloc privatization of the INOC is such a bold departure that it would create very substantial domestic and regional resistance and could undermine coherent national policy making, whereas the partial privatization through PSAs would be more acceptable and effective on both these grounds. Of the public decentralized models, full-blown decentralization of ownership on a regional basis would add to politically centrifugal forces. A decentralization of operations or, more likely an 'unbundling' in the form of component spin-offs, might achieve some of the same hoped for benefits of economically and even politically invigorating the periphery, without threatening political fragmentation. Finally, the private decentralized option offers a variety of advantages, including that it can be employed in incremental fashion, although the complexity of its management would be a major challenge.

Summary Assessment

An academic, political economy perspective does not necessarily accord with political reality. Instead of considering all theoretically possible options, it makes more sense to point to only what appear to be the most politically feasible models of allocation and ownership, and mixes of them, for purposes of a summary evaluation.

Although Iraqis obviously do not constitute a homogenous political actor, as regards policy toward the oil industry, with the exception of the single but important issue of regional control over oilfields, they are less heterogeneous in regard to oil than their mix of religions, ethnicities and political commitments might suggest. It is not misleading, therefore, to speak of an Iraqi position in general terms, providing qualification where required. The majority of Iraqis appear to favour public options for ownership, whether centralized as at present, or decentralized by virtue of being 'unbundled.'[1] A

---

1. Adnan Pachachi, a prominent, liberal member of the Iraqi Governing Council, stated in July 2003 at a meeting of the US Council on Foreign Relations that his support for privatization of inefficient state enterprises did not apply to the oil sector. Islamists, both Sunni and Shiʻa, also support continuation of public ownership of oil out of their reading of

fewer number of Iraqis would countenance privatization through PSAs and probably still fewer would support immediate, direct private decentralization in the form of privatizations of even downstream components, to say nothing of upstream ones. Kurds and some Shi'ites, especially those based in Basra and loyal to the Supreme Council for the Islamic Revolution in Iraq (SCIRI), who see decentralization of ownership to a regional or provincial level as ideal, evinced hesitation in pushing this demand prior to the August 2005 negotiations over the constitution. Whether their escalated demands at that time for regional/provincial control over all newly developed oilfields were part of a bargaining strategy or reflected a genuine, steadfast commitment, is impossible to know.

Iraqi preferences for the allocation of oil revenues seem more mixed. The Iraqi National Accord, which was a key actor leading up to the invasion, is on record as supporting a Development Board model. Iraqis more generally would probably endorse either a social safety net or allocations to individuals, a la Alaska. Political elites representing Kurds and Shi'ites have argued in favour of decentralization of allocations to regional levels, albeit on the basis of population, a position that those representing Sunni interests on the constitutional committee of the National Assembly appeared to accept.

These putative preference distributions suggest possible compromise solutions, whereby the various Iraqi parties receive at least some of their hoped for outcomes. So, for example, possible

---

the shari'a, in which 'open minerals,' such as salt, sulphur, asphalt and oil cannot be privately owned. Members of the political elite generally and Governing Council specifically who are inclined to support some form of privatization will be cautious about publicly endorsing it, lest they be seen as puppets of the Occupying Powers.

tensions between 'centralists' and 'regionalists' (e.g., Sunnis v. Kurds and some Shi'ites, especially those based in the South), might be ameliorated through a combination of continued centralized ownership, maybe coupled with 'unbundling,' with allocations being decentralized to regions, provinces, or individuals through revenue sharing and/or social safety net or personal allocation systems.

Over the long term democratization, economic growth and societal improvement are all likely to be maximized by approaches that deconcentrate the oil industry sectorally and geographically, while spreading its ownership beyond the bounds of the state, whose prerogative to set overall national policy should remain intact and even be enhanced. The structure of and rewards provided by the oil industry will contribute more to the balance between centre-periphery political and governmental relations than any other aspect of the economy. Clearly that balance has historically been too favourable to the centre, but a radical, sudden realignment of power toward the periphery could be politically and economically deleterious. Although the needs of Iraq are manifold and pressing, a gradualist approach to vital economic and political questions is essential if key decisions are to be accepted as legitimate and if temporary measures are not to restrict future policy options.

As regards ownership, an approach that paves the way for deconcentration and privatization, without forcing this second step, is that of an incremental 'unbundling,' whereby functional and possibly geographical companies are spun off from the INOC and the Ministry of Oil. Some of those companies, operating under general policy guidelines and Iraqi law, might at some stage enter into agreements with international oil companies

(IOCs) for service contracts or PSAs, but such decisions would not need to be made immediately, nor should they be, given the need for a recognized and legitimate Iraqi government as a precondition for the engagement of international financial institutions, companies and others. Some portion of oil revenues could be earmarked to facilitate ultimate Iraqi private ownership of these unbundled companies. In these matters the Algerian and Mexican cases might be particularly instructive. As in these examples, unbundling can be done in incremental fashion and be coupled with or separated from privatization through PSAs or, hypothetically, the establishment of joint ventures. In addition to being incremental, this unbundling approach can help to avoid a winner take all situation because it can spread benefits relatively widely, possibly being used in creative ways, for example, to ensure balance between the centre and periphery.

Finally, as regards allocations, the major challenges will be to ensure that whatever arrangements are used to overcome short term problems (widespread poverty and desperate needs for health and other human welfare services and possibly the need to buy general political support and legitimacy) do not prejudice the state's long term capacity to manage the economy, nor civil society's capacities to play a leading role in the society and polity. As with the case of ownership, this in turn suggests that approaches that permit incremental decision making and which distribute resources relatively widely, while retaining a key policy making role for the state, are to be preferred. Locking away significant shares of oil earnings in nonrenewable resource funds or establishing permanent revenue sharing arrangements do not seem particularly advisable approaches.

Appendices

Appendix A: Lessons Learned From Decentralization Programmes

Since the early 1980s many African and Asian countries have started a process of transferring both power and resources to their sub-national governments. It is seen as a means to promote democracy and expand participation in decision making. Some countries, like Ethiopia and Uganda, have moved quickly, whereas others, like Sudan and Indonesia, with more intricate political problems, including the vital one of oil revenue sharing, have made less progress.

Recent studies have indicated that decentralization can reduce poverty both directly, through better targeting to regions/ individuals with greatest needs and indirectly, through increased efficiency of provisioning of public services. Fiscal decentralization in Africa typically leads to a shift from local expenditures on administration to those on health and education, but current expenditures (salaries) tend to absorb most of the increases. African countries are particularly prone to capture by local interests and local governments often have very limited taxing powers, leading to dependency on transfers from the central government. In general, recent cross-country studies point to two essential components that determine the success of fiscal decentralization in achieving social service delivery and poverty alleviation targets: (i) strong revenue raising and administrative capacity at the local level and (ii) successful political decentralization, which enables local communities to influence policy making.

Countries that have embarked on decentralization programmes include:

Ethiopia

The process of fiscal decentralization was initiated in 1992. Providing local governments with additional autonomy was widely seen as a way to unite the ethnically fragmented country, while delegating to them the task of solving their own economic problems. In the past several years the amount of resources devoted to local governments has increased and their delivery of health and education services has improved. Three important factors have contributed to this relative success: A fairly robust and extensive framework to support decentralization; capacity building at the sub-national level; a significant intergovernmental transfer programme.

Uganda

Since the implementation of fiscal decentralization in 1993, poverty appears to have fallen markedly in Uganda, with the proportion of Ugandans living in poverty falling from 55.5 per cent in 1992 to about 44.0 per cent in 1997. Regional poverty has declined as well. These improvements emanated from state policies, which have focused on education and healthcare, as well as socially related sectors including agriculture and water. Decentralization has improved the services provided to the poor in addition to encouraging a higher degree of involvement at the local level. In particular, recent reports suggest that the efficiency of the police force and civil service is improved. There is a continuing inability, however, to generate local revenues or to establish sufficient accountability.

Sudan

Proclamations were issued in 1995 increasing the number of states from nine to twenty-six and defining powers and revenue-sharing agreements between the federal and state governments. Analysis of the evolution in budgetary outlays on education, health and water indicate that after more than five years of fiscal decentralization, total spending on social sectors is still very low. Decentralization has not led to a substantial improvement in social service delivery and although some indicators such as infant mortality, malnutrition and adult illiteracy have shown slight improvements, most other crucial ones have either stagnated or even deteriorated. Most alarming is the apparent deterioration in the primary school enrolment, child immunization and incidence of infectious diseases. In addition to a shortage in funding, the effectiveness of decentralization is reduced by lack of managerial expertise at the sub-national levels and by the fact that Sudan is still affected by conflict.

Indonesia

Beginning in 2001, the central government replaced many existing grants from the centre to the regions with a 'general allocation grant' and those regions with substantial resource sectors (including oil) began to receive a share of the revenues accruing from their exploitation. This decentralization was intended to address some of the grievances of Indonesia's regions, which culminated in the eruption of violence in several parts of the country after President Soeharto left office in May 1999. The changes embodied in the legislation were to permit the resource-rich regions to retain a greater share of profits from the exploitation of natural resources within their borders.

Although it is too early to judge the success of the changes that effectively took place in 2001, many observers note the following problems: (i) the move from a tightly centralized and authoritarian regime to a more decentralized one appears to have reproduced corruption at the local level; (ii) because local governments do not have revenue raising powers, they revert to illegal taxes on interregional trade in order to cope with new expenditure responsibilities; and (iii), given the constraint on central government budgets, the poorer states suffer from reduced central government grants as a result of decentralization reforms that favour resource rich states.

Lessons learned from these cases suggest that in addition to assigning expenditure and revenue responsibilities among the different levels of government, the fiscal decentralization process should ensure that sub-national policy making autonomy also exits and that there should be clarity in the roles and responsibilities between the central and the local governments. Decentralization should be complemented with measures to increase revenue-raising capacity at the central level and to harmonize tax policies between the states in order to prevent competitive behavior amongst them, which ultimately reduces revenue mobilization. Finally, decentralization should be aimed at the levels of government, which have the necessary administrative capacity. Authorities should ensure that capacity building and strengthening of state financial management are part of the process.

Appendix B: Revitalizing Agriculture

One important recipient of present and future oil revenues should be the country's rural areas, where 30 per cent of the population live, including a significant number of the poorer Shi'ites. These areas have been devastated in recent years by regime policies, international sanctions, and the detrimental impact on food production of the UN oil-for-food initiative. This woeful legacy could be compounded were power to control the countryside devolved to tribal shaikhs and other strongmen in the form of preferential access to credit, water, and possibly the land of their Ba'thi predecessors.

At present there is a severe shortage of vital inputs like seed, credit, spare parts for tractors, etc, made worse by a serious degradation of the irrigation systems south of Baghdad and difficulties in accessing urban markets because of damage to transport systems. A further complicating factor is a labour shortage in rural areas exacerbated by the departure of foreign workers. It must also be supposed that in many instances title to the land itself is in dispute, making it difficult to use as security for any but the most extortionate of local loans.

The immediate priority must be to encourage an emphasis

on raising agricultural output by two forms of intervention: the provision of credit, seed and other inputs; and the institution of subsidies sufficient to raise prices enough to encourage farmers and peasants to start producing again. Over the medium and long terms linkages with the industrial sector, particular those components capable of providing locally produced fertilizers, pesticides and spare parts for agricultural machinery, should be promoted.

A basic problem will be how to deliver agricultural inputs and credit quickly and fairly throughout the rural sector. In some districts, it may be possible to make use of what remains of the agricultural service and marketing cooperatives established to promote the land reform of the 1960s and 1970s. In others there may still be local branches of the agricultural cooperative bank, but in some there may be no alternative to establishing new agricultural councils of some sort. While such delivery mechanisms would not be very satisfactory from either the point of view of efficiency or equity, they could help to meet an immediate need while allowing time for more market-oriented institutions to be established. A temporary initiative of this nature should be announced to last for a finite period - two or three years - during which time new rural institutions can be developed to target individual farmers. This would also provide time to begin to address the problem of private property in land, an issue that can only be finally settled by a combination of a new cadastral survey and the establishment of a proper legal/judicial system.

Appendix C: Unbundling Oil Services in Algeria

The Algerian state oil company, Sonatrach, is named for the industry's major activities running from upstream down (the

'Société Nationale pour la Recherche, la Production, le Transport, la Transformation, et la Commercialisation des Hydrocarbures'), literally embodies the ideal of a vertically integrated oil and gas company. After 1971, when Algeria nationalized remaining French petroleum assets, Sonatrach also assumed the state's triple role as owner of the mineral resources, promoter of investments in the hydrocarbons sector, and protector of public interests.

After President Boumediene's death in 1978, President Chadly Ben Jadid's sought to bring Sonatrach – and its oil rents – under closer supervision by means of a National Energy Council chaired by the President of the Republic and including the prime minister and various other high government and party officials. In order the better to control the corporate giant, the government divided it in the early 1980s into some fifteen autonomous public sector companies. The company in charge of refining and distribution was further subdivided in 1987 into Naftec and Naftal, to manage Algeria's refineries and distribution systems (including privately owned gas stations), respectively. Naftal subsequently lost its state monopoly, but Algeria's pricing system has discouraged any potential foreign competitors from entering the local market. Upstream, autonomous public sector companies managed well servicing (ENSP), well maintenance (ENTP), plant construction (GTP), civil engineering and construction (GCB), drilling (ENAFOR), pipelines (ENAC), engineering design (ENEP), and geophysical surveys (ENAGEO).

Under pressure from trade union, the National Energy Council, which had itself undergone various political permutations since its founding in 1981, reversed the de-integration of the industry in 1998. The various public sector companies created in the

1980s were restored to the mother corporation. Even on paper, however, twenty years of vertical de-integration has left its mark on Sonatrach. The companies retain some organizational identity as subsidiaries of the parent company, and most of the upstream service companies are only 51 per cent owned by Sonatrach. Equity management companies that might in theory privatize them hold their remaining shares. ENAGEO, the geophysical survey company, could be a prime candidate, for foreign companies working in Algeria perceive it to be a useful partner having state of the art technology. Presently there are discussions within Sonatrach about setting up a venture capital company to 'hive off' some of its employees into oil-related businesses, such as service companies. During the Boumediene years service units had gained experience through Sonatrach's joint ventures with foreign firms. Engineering services, for instance, benefited from Condor, a joint venture between Sonatrach and Brown and Root (Halliburton) that the Chadly regime abolished. Current plans to privatize public sector enterprises, however, whether in hydrocarbons or other sectors, are on hold.

Ambitious plans to restructure Sonatrach are also on hold. Energy Minister Chekib Khelil's draft law of 3 September 2002, calls for stripping Sonatrach of its government functions, a vision shared within the company management even by those who opposed Khelil's specific plans. Former CEO Abdelhak Bouhafs, a leader of the 'modernization' movement within the corporation, claims that the management 'want Sonatrach to have the status purely of an oil and gas company, stripped of government functions, and exercising its full capacity of initiative and responsiveness.'[1]

---

1. Ali Aissaoui, *The Political Economy of Oil and Gas*, Oxford: Oxford University Press, 2001. p. 219.

Khelil's draft law would establish two independent state authorities respectively to 'assure non-discriminatory access to investors' in concluding production and exploration contracts and to monitor technical regulations and pipeline concessions. Sonatrach would then compete on a level playing field with foreign companies for product sharing contracts and other arrangements. A clause in the draft bill enables Sonatrach to 'back in' with up to a 25 per cent share in contracts negotiated with other companies. The basic intent of the proposed legislation is to encourage greater foreign investment, but critics view it as opening the door to a possible privatization of Sonatrach, an accusation denied by the minister. The draft bill would, however, end Sonatrach's monopoly in the transport sector and positively encourage competition downstream by liberalizing end-user prices.[1]

---

1.   www.mem-algeria.org/legis/index.htm

Biographical Notes

Clement M. Henry is a professor in the Department of Government at the University of Texas at Austin. He has received a Fulbright, Ford and a variety of other grants to assist his research in the Middle East and North Africa. His publications include *The Politics of Islamic Finance*, co-edited with Rodney Wilson; *Globalization and the Politics of Development in the Middle East*, co-authored with Robert Springborg; *The Mediterranean Debt Crescent* and, under the name of Clement Henry Moore, *Images of Development: Egyptian Engineers in Search of Industry*, *Politics in North Africa*, and *Tunisia Since Independence: The Dynamics of One-Party Rule*. His courses and resources are online at www.la.utexas.edu/chenry and some of his articles and recent papers are available at http://www.la.utexas.edu/~chenry/vitae.html.

Massoud Karshenas is Professor of Economics at the School of Oriental and African Studies (SOAS), University of London. He is the external coordinator of research on social policy in the Middle East and North Africa region at the United Nations Research Institute for Social Development and a Research Fellow of the Economic Research Forum. Recent publications include *Social Policy in the Middle East: Economic, Political and Gender Dynamics* (with Valentine Moghadam) and *Global Poverty Estimates and the Millennium Goals: Towards a Unified Framework*.

Roger Owen is currently the A. J. Meyer Professor of Middle East History at Harvard University and a former director of Harvard's Center for Middle Eastern Studies. He previously taught Middle East political and economic history at Oxford University where he was also the Director of St Antony's College Middle East Centre. Publications include *Cotton and the Egyptian Economy:1820-1914*, *The Middle East in the World Economy:1800-1914*, *State, Power and Politics in the Making of the Modern Middle East* (third edition) and *Lord Cromer: Victorian Imperialist, Edwardian Proconsul*, a biography of Evelyn Baring, the first Lord Cromer. He has written a regular column for the Arabic newspaper, *al-Hayat*, since the late 1980s and one for the *al-Ahram Weekly* (Cairo) since 1999.

Mona Said is Lecturer in Economics at SOAS and is involved in the research activities of the London Middle East Institute. She holds a PhD in Economics from the University of Cambridge. Previous publications and current research interests are in the areas of labour and human resource economics, public finance, growth and macroeconomic policy, poverty and income distribution and analysis of structural adjustment programs.

John Sfakianakis is Chief Economist of the Saudi British Bank. Previously, he served as Chief Regional Economist and Senior Vice President of Samba Financial Group, Riyadh, Saudi Arabia. He has also been an advisor to the United Nations Development Programme (UNDP) and to the Minister of Economy and Planning, Riyadh, Saudi Arabia. He has worked with the World Bank Group, Washington D.C., in the East Asia, Human Development and Middle East departments and has taught at Harvard University and the American University in Cairo. He has published extensively on economic topics in the Middle East.

Robert Springborg holds the MBI Al Jaber Chair in Middle East Studies at SOAS and is Director of the London Middle East Institute. He has worked as a consultant for USAID, the US State Department, the UNDP, and UK government departments including the Foreign and Commonwealth Office, the Ministry of Defence and the Department for International Development. He has held academic positions at Macquarie University in Sydney, Australia; the University of California, Berkeley; the University of Pennsylvania and the University of Sydney. His publications include *Mubarak's Egypt: Fragmentation of the Political Order*, *Family, Power and Politics in Egypt*, *Globalization and the Politics of Development in the Middle East* (co-authored with Clement M. Henry) and several editions of the co-authored textbook *Politics in the Middle East*.

Bibliography

Ahmed, Ehtisham and Raju Singh, 'Political Economy of Oil-Revenue Sharing in a Developing Country: Illustrations from Nigeria', *IMF Working Paper*, International Monetary Fund, January 2003.

Biblawi, Hazem, 'The Rentier State in the Arab World', in Giacomo Luciani, ed., *The Arab State*, Berkeley: University of California Press, 1990.

Bremer, L. Paul with Malcolm McConnell, *My Year in Iraq*, New York: Simon & Schuster, 2006.

Carnegie Endowment for International Peace, 'From Victory to Success: Afterwar Policy in Iraq', *Foreign Policy and Carnegie Endowment Special Report*, 2003.

Chehab, Zaki, *Iraq Ablaze: Inside the Insurgency*, London: I.B. Tauris, 2005.

Daniel, Philip, prepared, n.d., *Petroleum Revenue Management, an Overview*, World Bank, ESMAP Programme.

Diamond, Larry, *Squandered Victory: The American Occupation and the Bungled Effort to Bring Democracy to Iraq*, New York: Times Books, 2005.

Djerejian, Edward P. and Frank G. Wisner (Co-Chairs), Rachel Bronson and Andrew S. Weiss (Project Co-Directors), 'Guiding Principles for U.S. Post-Conflict Policy in Iraq', *Report of an Independent Working Group Cosponsored by the Council on Foreign*

Relations and the James A. Baker III Institute for Public Policy of Rice University, New York: Council on Foreign Relations, 2002.

Dodge, Toby, *Iraq's Future: The Aftermath of Regime Change*, London: International Institute for Strategic Studies, March 2005.

Dodge, Toby and Steven Simon (eds), *Iraq at the Crossroads: State and Society in the Shadow of Regime Change*, London: International Institute for Strategic Studies, 2003.

Etherington, Mark, *Revolt on the Tigris: The Al-Sadr Uprising and the Governing of Iraq*, London: Hurst & Co, 2005.

Gelb, Alan, *Oil Windfalls: Blessing or Curse?*, New York: Oxford University Press, 1988.

Ghai, Yash, Mark Lattimer and Yahia Said, *Building Democracy in Iraq*, London: Minority Rights Group International, 2003.

Hashim, Ahmed, *Insurgency and Counter-Insurgency in Iraq*, London: Hurst & Co, 2005.

International Crisis Group (ICG), *Can Local Governance Save Central Government?*, 27 October 2004.

International Crisis Group (ICG), *Governing Iraq*, 25 August.

Jabar, Faleh A., 2005, 'The Constitution of Iraq: Religious and Ethnic Relations', *Micro Study: Minority Rights and Conflict Prevention*, Minority Rights Group International, December 2003.

Jabar, Faleh Abdul and Hosham Dawod (eds), *Tribes and Power: Nationalism and Ethnicity in the Middle East*, London: Saqi Books, 2003.

Marcel, Valerie, 'The Future of Oil in Iraq: Scenarios and Implications', *The Royal Institute of International Affairs, Sustainable Development Programme, Briefing Paper,* December 2002.

Murphey, Richard (Chair), C. Richard Nelson (Rapporteur), 'Winning the Peace: Managing a Successful Transition in Iraq', *Policy Paper*, American University, Washington D.C. and The Atlantic Council of the United States, January 2003.

Phillips, David L., *Losing Iraq: Inside the Postwar Reconstruction Fiasco*, London: Westview Press, 2005.

Rathmell, Andrew, 'Planning Post-conflict Reconstruction in Iraq: What Can We Learn?', *International Affairs*, vol. 81, no. 5, 2005.

Ross, Michael L., 'The Political Economy of the Resource Curse',

World Politics, vol. 51, no. 2, January 2005, pp. 297–322.

Ross, Michael L., 'Does Oil Hinder Democracy?', *World Politics*, vol. 53, no. 3, April 2001, pp. 325–261.

Tripp, Charles, 'The United States and State-building in Iraq', *Review of International Studies*, vol. 30, 2004, pp. 545–58.

The James A. Baker III Institute for Public Policy of Rice University, 'Social, Cultural, and Religious Factors that Influence Oil Supply and Foreign Relations with the Middle East', *Cultural Workshop Seminar Report*, 1 November 2002.

Index

Sudan 103, 105
Sunnis 19, 27, 57, 64, 84, 99, 100
Supreme Council for the Islamic
　Revolution in Iraq (SCIRI) 99

Texas 35, 38
Tunisia 45, 60

Uganda 103, 104–5
UK *see* United Kingdom
UN *see* United Nations
United Kingdom
　Adam Smith Institute 63
　BBC 'Newsnight' 9n.1 and 2
　DFID 30–1, 32
United Nations
　oil-for-food programme 34, 107
　Security Council 76
United States
　Agency for International
　　Development 50
　Army Corps of Engineers 19
　Bush Administration 9n.1 and 2
　Council on Foreign Relations 98n.1
　Heritage Foundation 9n.1, 63, 90,
　　92

invasion of Iraq 7–8
Memorandum of Law (1976) 36
New American Foundation 64
oil policies of 9
Texas 38
USAID 50
Unocal 10
US *see* United States
USAID 50

West Bank 45
West Qurna field 88
Wilde, Anna 32
Wolfowitz, Paul 13
World Bank 33n.1, 44, 46, 47n.1,
　48n.1, 56, 74n.1
World Economic Forum (Amman
　2003) 39, 61

Yemen 45, 56

About the London Middle East Institute

The London Middle East Institute (LMEI) of SOAS is a charitable, tax-exempt organisation whose purpose is to promote knowledge of all aspects of the Middle East, both among the general public and to those with special interests in the region. Drawing on the expertise of over seventy SOAS academic Middle East specialists, accessing the substantial library and other resources of SOAS, and interacting with over 300 individual and corporate affiliates, the LMEI since its founding in 2002 has sponsored conferences, seminars and exhibitions; conducted training programmes; and undertaken consultancies for public and private sector clients. The LMEI publishes a monthly magazine – *The Middle East in London* – and with Saqi it publishes four books annually in the SOAS Middle East Issues series. These activities are guided by a Board of Trustees on which is represented SOAS, the British Academy, the University of London, the Foreign and Commonwealth Office and private sector interests.

Professor Robert Springborg

MBI Chair in Middle East Studies
Director, London Middle East Institute
School of Oriental and African Studies
Russell Square, London WC1H 0XG
United Kingdom
www.lmei.soas.ac.uk